Autobiography of J(*Hall*

Second Edition

Born 14 Jan 1882, Escalante, Utah
Died 4 Jan, 1966, St. George, Utah

Transcribed by his grandson,
George Franklin Reid,
January 1997, Roy, Utah.

Copyright

Autobiography of Job Franklin Hall
Second Edition

Original manuscript transcribed and edited by his grandson,
George Franklin Reid

Job and Annie (Clove) Hall at about the time they were married. Their daughter, Grace Hall Reid, says her mother had a beautiful white dress for this photo, but it was not the wedding dress.

History of Job F. Hall

I am a literal decendant of George Hall and his wife Mary, (Williams?) who came to America from England (Dorchester?) about 1630, and settled first at Dorchester, Mass. but a short time later, in company with Nicholas White, Ezra Dean, Walter Dean, Wm. Hotherell, a mr Leonard, and others the Town of Taunton, Mass. was settled and an Iron works, called "a Bloomery", was established which George Hall operated on a lease till his death when his son John hue Hall took over the management for the balance of his life.

George Halls oldest son, Samuel married Nicholas Whites oldest daughter Elyabeth. Their son Ebenezer, married Jane Bumpus and moved to Maine. He was killed by Indians on Matinicus Island. I am decended through this line, being the Son of Wm. H. Hall, son of Job Potter Hall, who was the son of Ebenezer Hall, son of Ebenezer Hall who was the Son of Ebenezer Hall and Jane Bumpus.

I was born in a "dugout" in the north side of the Bench Escalante, Utah is built on. This Bench is about 15 or 20 feet higher than the Escalante Creek or River. There was about 2 feet of snow on the ground when I was born, on the 14th of January 1882. I was the 4th son and so increased the Family membership to six. Six people in a small room,

Facsimile of the first page of his history in his own handwriting.

4

Contents

Transcriber's Note to the First Edition

The Following autobiography was written many years ago by my grandfather, Job Franklin Hall, in his own hand with pencil on lined paper. The yellowing sheets are filled both sides with his clear and expressive writing, telling of some of his life's events. It seems odd that he would hand write it because he was a good typist and typed many letters and documents for business and church work. Judging by a few comments he makes, such as certain houses standing in 1957, I assume he wrote it about that time or the following year.

He has divided his history into categories to make it clearer. The first is a short history of his ancestors followed by some history of his own life and feelings. This is followed by the categories of church work, scouting, music, public offices held, work and then as an afterthought he added many pages of miscellaneous. Because these miscellaneous items mostly occur during his early years I have taken the liberty of placing it right after the main history and then followed it with the other parts. This is out of the order in which he wrote it but it adds so much to round out his personality and set the ground work for the parts which follow.

The manuscript was typed into a computer file for publication and follows the original as far as it is readable. I have retained all original spellings of names and places and the sentence structure, only correcting any obvious misspelled common words, which were very few - he was a good speller! Some words have been added in [brackets] to clarify the meaning. gfr

Note to the Second Edition

I first transcribed his hand-written history over ten years ago and it was only published locally and copies sent out to the family. Since then I have written and published many books on Amazon KDP and decided to reissue this book. This way many more family members and descendants will have access to it.

I have changed the text font and made the pages smaller than the original 8-1/2x11 to this 7x10 size with full one-column paragraphs instead of the original two-column book.

The same text is included without changes and the original pictures have been added in at the appropriate locations.

G. Franklin Reid
January 2024
Logan, Utah

History of Job F. Hall

I am a literal decendant of George Hall and his wife Mary (Williams?) who came to America from England (Dorchester?) about 1630, and settled first at Dorchester, Mass. but a short time later, in company with Nicholas White, Ezra Dean, Walter Dean, Wm Wetherell, a mr Leonard, and others the Town of Taunton, Mass. was settled and an Iron works called "a Bloomery", was established which George Hall operated on a lease till his death, when his son John Hall took over the management for the balance of his life.

George Halls oldest son, Samuel married Nicholas Whites oldest daughter Elizabeth. Their son Ebenezer, married Jane Bumpus and moved to Maine. He was killed by Indians on Matinicus Island. I am decended through this line, being the son of Wm H. Hall, son of Job Pitcher Hall, who was the son of Ebenezer Hall, son of Ebenezer Hall who was the son of Ebenezer Hall and Jane Bumpus.

I was born in a "dugout" in the north side of the Bench Escalante, Utah is built on. This Bench is about 15 or 20 feet higher than the Escalante Creek or River. There was about 2 feet of snow on the ground when I was born, on the 14th of January, 1882. I was the 4th son and so increased the family membership to six. Six people in a small room.

Facsimle of first page of Job F. Hall's history. It is hand-written on the standard note-book paper of that day. An 8x10, two-hole lined paper.

Image has been reduced to fit on this page.

Part 1 – History of Job F. Hall

I am a literal descendant of George Hall and his wife, Mary (Williams?) who came to America from England (Dorchester about 1630 and settled first at Dorchester, Massachusetts. But a short time later in company with Nicholas White, Ezra Dean, Walter Dean, Wm. Witherall, a mister Leonard and others, the town of Taunton, Massachusetts was settled and an iron works, called a "Bloomery", was established which George Hall operated on a lease till his death, when his son, John Hall took over the management for the balance of his life.

George Hall's oldest son, Samuel, married Nicholas White's oldest daughter, Elizabeth. Their son Ebenezer married Jane Bumpus and moved to Maine. He was killed by Indians on Matinicus Island. I am descended through this line, being the son of Wm. Wesley Hall and Malinda Hunt. She was the daughter of Amos Hunt and Nancy Garret Welborn, converts to the Church from Mucklinberg [or Muhlenberg] County, Kentucky.

[My father, William Wesley Hall was the] son of Job Pitcher Hall who was the son of Ebenezer Hall, son of Ebenezer Hall who was the son of Ebenezer Hall and Jane Bumpus.

I was born in a "dugout" [home] in the north side of the bench [which] Escalante, Utah is built on. This bench is about 15 or 20 feet higher than the Escalante Creek or River. There was about 2 feet of snow on the ground when I was born on the 14th of January, 1882. I was the 4th son and so increased the family membership to six. Six people in a small room dug out near the foot of the hill on the north side.

I spent the winter of 1914-15 in Escalante and on Jan 14th, 1915 I went and took a look at my birthplace. The mound of earth and small cavity in the hillside indicated where the dugout had been. There was about 18 inches of snow on the ground, a north breeze blowing, and it was very cold. Not a pleasant looking place to have been born[!].

All my younger days were spent in Escalante with the exception of a year near Teasdale or Thurber, in what was then known as Rabbit Valley. My father[, William Wesley Hall] lost a good wheat crop that year by having it get frozen, so he returned to Escalante. We lived on a farm about 4 miles west of Escalante most of the time, so I didn't get to go to school till I was 8 years old. But my father had taught me to read and write and to "cipher" as it was called then, so when I did go to school I was soon at the head of the class. My first teacher was "Aunt Susan White", a noted teacher of her time. I spent part of a few other years in school there. The teachers I remember are Wm. Thompson, Paddy Miles and George Dodds. My father continued to teach me in the intervals. I believe this was good for me as it taught me to study things our for myself to a great extent.

When I was about 13 year old my father traded our farm for a herd of sheep and moved to the new town of Enterprise, Utah. He had spent some time as a young man in this area, so knew of the wonderful land there, and the chances of water for it. I went to school part of the first year at the old town of Hebron, Gera Terry was the teacher. The next three winters I went to school in Hebron, being so fortunate as to have for my teacher, Eugene Schoppman, one of the most, if not the most noted teachers ever to teach school in Southern Utah. Beside the regular grade school course I studied bookkeeping and accounting, elocution, astronomy, and mathematics under Schoppman in the night school he conducted. These studies were a great help to me in later life.

It was several years after our settlement at Enterprise before the water was gotten out onto the land so we were forced to seek work away from home a good share of the time to make a living. I worked as a farm hand in Pine Valley, Utah at Holt's Ranch and Terry's Ranch. Worked on the railroad when the Utah, San Pedro and Salt Lake road was built from Milford, Utah to Uvada, on the Utah-Nevada line. This is now the main line of the Union Pacific between Salt Lake City and San Pedro [(Los Angeles)], California.

I herded sheep, sheared sheep, dipped sheep, worked at the carpenter trade with my father whenever he got any work of this kind to do. Chopped cord wood, [and] logging and mining timber at the old mining camp at State Line, Utah. Chopped mining timber for the mine at Delamar, Nevada in the mountains south of Clover Valley, Nevada. Worked on the brick yard at Enterprise as an offbearer [of bricks] and helped burn the brick. Helped burn lime, worked on the Enterprise Reservoir and on the canals. Chopped posts and built fences. Freighted, and did everything honorable anyone else did in the west for a living.

In early spring of 1903 my brother, Wm. E. Hall, who was camp boss for Hendrickson Bros. of Glenwood, Utah, wrote me to come and trail a herd of sheep through the mountains from Milford, Utah to Glenwood. So I met him at Milford and trailed this herd through. After shearing I took the "drys" (yearlings and weathers)[(male sheep that had been "cut" or neutered - GHR)] of four herds up into the mountains east of Glenwood and herded them through the summer. Was at the head of Gooseberry Creek at Brown's Hole, on Shingle Mill Creek and at Fish Lake on the U. M. Mountains.

About the middle of August I quit and went to Hatch on the Sevier River above Panguitch where my sister, Mary, and the girl I was engaged to lived. I worked there building a big barn for Jos. Barnhurst and on the ranch for Sam Barnhurst the balance of the summer and early fall.

In October, I took Annie M. Clove to St. George, Utah, and married her in the St. George L.D.S. Temple. David Cannon, Pres. of the temple performing the ceremony. We spent a few days in Enterprise visiting with my father and mother, brothers and sisters, relatives and friends, letting them get acquainted with the wonderful girl I had married, then returned to Hatch to make our home. I had bought a lot and built a small house on it to live in. I built a large home for Sam Barnhurst that winter as well as several barns and worked for him most of the next summer. Some time, about the first of November of the year 1904 I got a letter from my father asking me to come and take over a mail route from Stateline, Utah, to Pioche, Nevada. It seems the contractor had "jumped" his contract and left, leaving the mail line on the hands of his bondsmen, B. J. Lund & Co., of Modena, Utah.

So I listened to his appeal and we moved to Stateline, Utah and took over this line. It was a star or pony route through the hills with two post offices between, one at Spring Valley and one at Ursine or Eagle Valley, Nevada. It was about 60 miles through, one way and I covered it [on] horseback, staying in Pioche one night and at Stateline the next, three trips each week. I changed horses at Eagle Valley. When spring came my brother-in-law, J. Z. Alger [probably John Zera Alger married to his sister, Mary Malinda] came and took the route over from me by previous arrangement. It was a cold winter and I wallowed [through] some deep snow over the Stateline Pass.

We went back to Hatch that spring and soon after I started a store in the kitchen of my home. It was sort of a branch of the

Garfield Exchange in Panquitch to start with as they furnished the merchandise at a wholesale price. I worked some for Sam Barnhurst, my wife's uncle, again this summer, and was appointed Postmaster for Hatch by the P.O. Department. That fall I went to work on the threshing machine, an old Nichols and Shepard Vibrator, 60 inch cylinder, 45 inch separator. This machine was run by a horse power that was run by six teams, (12 horses) hitched to sweepers, and traveling in a circle around the horse power. I had a team on this machine and cut bands for it. I did the same thing the next two threshing seasons.

In the spring of 1906 I began making preparations to build a store building across the street from where I was living. Before I got this building finished I got a call to go on a mission to the Southern States, so my father came and helped me get the building near enough finished so we could move the merchandise in[to] it before I left for the mission in December. He stayed and finished the building all up after I left.

I had been wallowing in snow 3 feet deep for a month doing this work, then went right down into Mississippi where it was warmer than it ever was in Hatch in mid-summer. As a result I contracted cystitis, which doctors knew little about at the time, so [I] was released in march because of illness and returned home. Dr. R. Garn Clark of Panguitch met the horse drawn stage when it arrived there about sun-up, and took me to his office and gave me some powders to take for the disease, and informed me to get sage brush leaves and soak them in cold water and drink a swallow before each meal and at bed time. He seemed to know what to do as I soon began to get better. He took me to my Aunt Mary Riding's home and told her to put me to bed in a dark room and let me sleep. She did this and my cousin, Job Riding and his wife took me home the next day. Job married Cassie Steel, daughter of Pres. M. M. Steel of the Panguitch Stake.

Dr. Clark's remedy worked so well that I was able to go to work in June, so I took a contract from the local Telephone Co. of Panquitch to get out 1,000 telephone poles and deliver them on their survey line from Panguitch to Orderville. I took a crew of men and went and helped get out these poles. We went first to the head of the East Fork of the Sevier River at what was called Blue Fly and cut and peeled Red Pine poles. When we got the poles distributed to Hatch we heard of a grove of lodge pole and Black Balsam trees that were fire kill and investigated this grove and found the poles good and access to them easy. So we finished the contract from there (this was Pole Canyon).

I got the most of this money, in a way, as all the men who helped me owed bills in the store and paid most of the money to me on their accounts. This money just about paid all the bills the store owed so it was a big help to me. Before this time I had paid the Garfield Exchange off and was buying goods from Salt Lake City and Ogden and Provo Farms. So [I] made several trips to Marys-vale for freight, either with my own team or going with the man who did the hauling. Also, we took grain in the store for merchan-dise and sold the oats to freight teams from Kane County and hauled the wheat to the gristmill in Panguitch and exchanged it for flour, Germade and other mill products which in turn were sold through the store.

When cold weather came on, my old bladder trouble came back so I sold the store and moved to Enterprise, as the doctor advised me to get into a lower altitude. This was the fall of 1907. In the spring of 1908 I had recovered my health sufficiently to work at the building trade, so I finished the home of Don Forsyth at New Castle, built a big barn for Steve Bunker in Grassvalley, and built a home for Jas. W. [or U.] Coleman. From this and several small jobs I saved enough money to go to school, so my wife and I went to Beaver in October and entered the Murdock Academy, which was then a branch of the B[righam] Y[oung] U[niversity] at Provo. Josiah E. Hickman was principal and I remember the following teachers: Rhinard Maeser, English, drama, rhetoric; Geo. H. Durhan, music and history; Miss Marnie Ollerton, English; Hettie White, domestic science; Mabel Frazer, art and domestic art; Fred Merril, agriculture and horticulture; Snyder, algebra & coach; Mr. Day algebra and history; Mr. May, science; Frank Pendleton, black-smithing & machine shop; John Henry Evans, book-keeping & ac-counting; John G. McQaurie [or McLuarie] , woodwork and religion.

There was an understanding between Prof. Hickman and I that I was to replace McQuarrie in the fall of 1909 as instructor in wood-work and religion. I was majoring in music and mathematics and was to teach in both of these depts. a few years later. But I got seri-ously injured working on the opera house, in Beaver, during the Christmas vacation and had to go home to Enterprise because of the injury and didn't return to school. Instead, I went to work for B. J. Lund & Co. in the store at Modena the last of March, 1909 and stayed on there most of the time for the next 3 years as bookkeeper and clerk. Here my knowledge of Spanish was useful.

In the fall of 1910, my brother-in-law, John Z. Alger, Jr., and I each filed on enlarged homesteads at the Point of Rocks. We bought a bunch of old ewes from Jas. A. Berry. That was the fall our first baby, Grace, was born -- on Nov. 11th, 1910. I was herding this bunch of sheep when Grace was born and when she was about a month old we went down on our dry farm and lived in a small 1-room house I had built so Annie could be with me while I was looking after these sheep. In the spring of 1911, I sold my interest in the sheep to Johnny [John Z. Alger, Jr.] and went to Lund, Utah and assisted in the construction of the store and warehouse for H. J. Co. Bob of St. George was the contractor. After the building was up I stayed and run the business for Mr. Doolittle. Annie came down and we stretched a curtain around one corner of the warehouse for kitchen and dining room and slept in one of the office rooms. Here I found more use for the Spanish language as most of our retail trade was from Mexican section hands.

During the three years I worked for Mr. Doolittle I became quite proficient in Spanish by hard and constant study so that I could make their invoices and statements in Spanish, which pleased them as they could see what they were charged with. I even made a sign in Spanish and attached it to the end of the building near the entrance which read, "Todo provisiones en esta tienda es muy barrato", meaning the price is very low on the merchandise in this store. This precipitated a humorous incident. Our competitor, J. David Leigh, thought this sign accounted for us getting most of the Mexican trade, so he had on e of the Mexicans make a sign for his store. After he put this sign up he got no Mexican trade. I don't remember the Spanish text but interpreted it said the goods were low grade, the prices too high and the owner was crooked. One section boss felt sorry for Leigh and advised him to remove it and told him what it meant.

Doolittle was a hard man to work for, a slave driver disposition and never satisfied with what one did, so I quit in the fall of 1912 and returned to Enterprise. The next spring I sold my home to Israel Pace, and traded my small farm to Joe and George Woodbury, getting a good team harness and wagon and several milk cows for it, built a larger house on the dry farm and moved down there. I shipped cream from the cows to pay living expenses and planted

14

about 10 acres of corn and a small patch of potatoes which both did well. We also furnished the New Castle Hotel with butter.

I took first prize on the potatoes grown there without irrigation at the county fair in Cedar City that year. The variety was Red Willards. I plowed about 20 acres [of] virgin land that fall and planted it to rye and got an excellent stand. The next spring I planted 25 acres of corn and some other crops which all grew fine till about the 6th of July, when a bad hail storm struck which beat the rye all out of the heads, as it was ripe and ready to cut, beat the leaves all off the corn and shredded the ears and left the field a shambles. Soon after this Mr. Doolittle came to the ranch and talked me into going back to Lund for him, promising me better treatment, a good house to live in and a raise in wages. So we moved back to Lund taking a cow with us to milk leaving the dry farm and team in the care of Annie's brother, Ivor Clove.

I got along fine with Mr. Doolittle for several months but finally his old domineering attitude returned and it was impossible to get along with him so I returned to the dry farm. Had better luck for a year after this as I got a contract to finish the north ditch for the New Castle Reclamation Co., which brought the water right by my ranch. I got a fresno and scooped out a big pond just below my field and bought and leased water from the Enterprise Reservoir so I could keep water in the pond and not have to haul water for my livestock.

Up until now it had been necessary to haul water in barrels to water my stock as well as for house use. This meant about 3 trips a week to the Holt mine well, about 1-1/2 miles away, and draw water by hand and fill six fifty-gallon barrels and haul them home and unload them. I got to be an expert at this and could unload them as the team moved forward slowly, and set the barrels out, touching each other in about 3 minutes. I had dug a well here, but it was 163 feet to water, and just about enough water for a team and a cow. Soon after getting this pond in operation, Ray Adams offered to by the place as headquarters for his sheep business, so I sold him the place and bought the old town[site] of Hebron with some of the adjoining fields, and moved my family, house and all up there. We had no water troubles here as the creek run[s] right through the farm, with one big spring about 100 yards from the house.

I now had about 12 head of cattle. We had just got settled here when Mr. Doolittle came again and talked me into going back to Lund. [He] said he couldn't find a bookkeeper that could keep his books straight like I had done and that if I would go back it would be as assistant manager, with no interference from him. We got along fine this time. He was in the hands of a receiver when I went back the second time and this caused a lot of friction. Thomas M. Holt was there then, representing Doolittle Company's creditors, and he wanted Doolittle to let me handle the finances of the company, as he felt that I was more conservative than Doolittle was, and that I could put the company back on its feet.

Doolittle objected to this, but Holt persisted until finally Doolittle gave in when Holt promised that if he would do this, he, Holt would leave and allow me to handle the business. This arrangement worked fine as far as finances were concerned and I soon had the company about out of debt. This rankled Doolittle and he made it so miserable for me that as soon as I had justified Holt's confidence in me I quit and left.

After I left the second time Doolittle incorporated the company and made it a stock company. He had sold some stock and among the stockholders was Mr. H. H Yeoman, who had been head of the Physic[s] Dept., of Princeton University, but was retired on a pension. He had bought $6,000.00 of preferred stock and was living in Lund when I returned this third time. He and I became very close friends and he taught me a lot of short cuts in mathematics. Mr. Doolittle and I had no trouble this time, but with a larger family (we had three children now) my salary just covered our living expenses.

I talked this matter over with Mr. Doolittle and explained the situation to him telling him that Lund was an unpleasant place to live in because the wind blew so much and the dust was so bad and fine that you couldn't shut it out of a room, and that unless I could be paid a large enough salary there to save up a little money I would be forced to leave as I couldn't afford to stay there for just a living, as I could make a living in places that were more pleasant to live in than Lund, Utah. He refused to give me a raise on acceptable terms so I quit.

I went to Escalante, Utah, that fall intending to buy an interest in my brothers store there but after a few months was convinced that the store wouldn't make a living for two families, so I returned to Enterprise. I had cut grain in the Enterprise fields the year before and did so again this grain cutting season. I have had some good team. With the team I had then I pulled a 6 foot McCormick binder all day long. These machines were made to be pulled with 3 horses.

About this time I was appointed Clerk of the Town Board of Enterprise and as clerk, put through a bond issue with the Palmer Bond & Mortgage Co. the money being used to complete the town's culinary water system. I served as clerk for several years.

In the spring of 1921, I traded my ranch at Old Hebron for about 1/3 of the Bastian Farm, east of Washington, Utah. While at Hebron I had built a good 4 room house, a good rock lined cellar with [a] rock floor, a good corral, stables and stock yard and had enclosed under one fence about 200 acres of land with 10 acres under separate fence for horse pasture. Had a good team and some good farm machinery and had accumulated 20 head of cattle the last year I was there, by [my daughter] Grace doing most of the plowing while I cleared land and with she and Priscilla helping with the seeding we raised 22 acres of corn without irrigation that averaged 56 bushels [of] shelled corn per acre. Also some potatoes and small grain and 5 acres Soudan grass [for hay]. But we were handicapped because of school. Grace rode a horse to Enterprise every day to school, some times in snow and bitter cold weather. And it was a constant worry. The horse she rode, though perfectly gentle, was high strung, so if she didn't come in sight of the ranch around the north end of Flat Top Mountain by about 4:30 p.m., I would get on another horse and go meet her.

The people of Hebron used to shuck corn on shares for Bro. George A. Holt for 1/6, to get a little corn to fatten a pig or two, yet I raised better corn without water at Hebron than Bro. Holt ever raised with water at his ranch where his corn was raised. Of course, I had become, by now, an expert dry farmer. The place I had traded for at Washington consisted of 30 acres of land, two-sevenths of the Bastian spring and all of a small spring north of the house that was brought down to the house through an open ditch. The improvements consisted of a 3 room adobe house and adobe grainery with cellar beneath and a corral. There was about an acre of old grape vineyard and about 3 acres of new orchard, some of which was about old enough to begin bearing. The children could walk to school here in good weather, about a mile, but in rainy weather I took them in my old Model T Ford [the car that Grace first drove at age 12 - GHR].

This is where I gained my first experience in scouting. I was sustained here as Scoutmaster in the fall of 1921. More will be said about it under "Scouting". I served here, too, as Clerk of the Town Board. I did a lot of carpenter work here, the most notable evidence being the home of "Id" (Israel, Jr.) Neilson just north of the highway on the west side of the creek. This was an old 1-1/2 story rock building with dormer windows in the roof and a small deck porch on the east. Under my supervision the roof and 1/2 story were taken off. New rooms built on the west and the present roof put on. I cut the rafters for this building while the wall were being laid up. This was such an unusual procedure that a great crowd gathered when we put the rafters on, and were very much surprised to find that everything fit. I am still proud of this building in 1957, as it looks good compared to all the modern buildings in this area.

The last year I lived here I went down on the Union Pacific railroad and worked on concrete bridges. J. F. and H. E. Schraoen of Salt Lake City and Ogden had the contract to replace all wood bridges with concrete from Rocks to the Dyke Siding, about 12 miles east of Las Vegas. Bill Hatton of Provo was our foreman. He was a very kind man. I went down there in Feb. 1923 and stayed until mid-July 1923. While here I had use for my first aid learned in scouting. As I was the only man in the group who had had this training, which I was called on to use several times.

Here, I learned concrete form building, steel reinforcement fabrication and a little knowledge of concrete finishing. These things proved very useful in later life. When I came home from there I made the trip alone in an old Model T Ford from the camp at Garnet, Nevada, to Washington, [Utah,] on the old wagon road through St. Thomas. I broke the front cross member on the car and had to gather rags from a junk heap and pack under the radiator to prevent puncturing it, and tie barbed wire across the lamp posts and twist it up to keep the front end together. Bought a new cross member in St. Thomas but the garage that sold it didn't have time to put it on, and the other garage refused to do it or let me have tools to do it because there was a feud between the two garages. So I had to run it on to Washington as it was.

In the fall of 1923, we sold the place at Washington and moved to St. George, where I went to work as a carpenter for Albert E. Miller, [the] leading contractor of St. George. We lost the place we first bought in St. George because of the failure of the man we sold the Washington property to and moved twice before we finally settled in the old home of Walter Dodge in the west side of St. George. I worked on a lot of homes in St. George and Santa Clara with Bro. Miller, but the most outstanding home of all is the home now owned by Dr. Richmond in the east side of St. George. this house was built for Emerald Cox in collaboration with Cal Dalton. When the Masons got ready to build in the gables, Cal couldn't cut the rafters. So Bob Worthen, on e of the brick-masons told Emerald that I could cut them because he knew I was writing articles on roof-framing for the American Builder when we roomed at Will McFarlane's home in Cedar City when we worked on the Bank of Southern Utah building there.

So, Emerald called me up and had me come down and cut the rafters. It is an intricate roof to cut as there are six different pitches in the roof, but the crown molding is carried on a level all around the building. This necessitated building some walls higher than others. My son-in-law, Whitney A. Cude, who is now stationed in Korea, helped me put the rafters on. Whitney is Naval Chief at the post in Korea. This house is one of the most beautiful homes in St. George now, 1957.

I went through a severe sick spell from May 15th to Dec. 1st, 1933. My father died of malignant cystitis in May 1933 and I seemed to have contracted the infection from waiting on him. We spent Christmas, 1933 with Whitney and [my daughter] Priscilla in Salt Lake City. While there I broadcast a few guitar selections over K.S.L. [Radio] on the Pathfinder program and promised to join the Utah Buckaroos that fall, but was too interested in mining in Nevada when fall came to join them. Priscilla's daughter, Dallas, was born there Jan 1st, 1943.

I had traveled for the Utah Woolen Mills part of the time for several years, so, as there was no building going on in St. George that spring, I took my samples and went to Pioche[, Nevada] on my regular schedule, but no one much was buying clothing at the close of the depression and I was barely making expenses. So when my brother-in-law, Everest Hackett offered me a job with him in his mine at Deerlodge[, Nevada, near Pioche] at $3.00 per day and board, I accepted it.

My wife joined me there in the spring and we spent over a year there while Mr. Hackett and I took out [of the mine] 2 or 3 car-loads of ore. Toward fall [of] 1935 Everest had to do some riding with his cattle and I went to Pioche to look for work. I got on as a carpenter at the C.C.C. Camp being built at Delmar's Ranch and went from there to Panaca, Nevada to build some chicken coops for Lafe Mathews.

I fell in love with Panaca and its people, so my wife joined me there where I found work at the carpenter trade to be quite steady.

19

I had arrived there just at the time people there and in Caliente and Pioche demanded something better than a shack to live in and I knew how to build it, so got steady work. We bought a lot with part of the money we got from the last car of ore we shipped from Deer-lodge, and built a large room to be used for a garage later and lived in that about two years, then I got R[ail] R[oad] ties and built a 4-room and bath home for us. About this time I bought 20 acres of land in the field north of Panaca with six shares of water. That was about a second foot of water for 24 hours every 8 days.

So now I started farming some on the side, using Lafe Mathews' team on a trade-work basis to do my plowing. A few years later I bought 80 acres of land in the White Wash area about three miles south of Panaca from the Arthur V. Lee estate together with six shares of water in the Panaca Irrigation Co. My son-in-law, Jack Reid came up from California that fall and we worked on the housing project at Castleton[, Nevada] that winter. When this building was done, Jack took over this farm but found that six shares didn't amount to much water after running so far, so he asked to be relieved of it.

I run both farms that summer but found that 5 or 6 miles was a long way to be moving machinery so sold the 20 acre farm to Kenneth Lee and Transferred the six shares of water out to the 80 acre farm. This gave me what was called 3 streams of water, nearly 3 second feet, 24 hours every 8 days. This was sufficient water for 30 or 40 acres of the land. I had bought an old Ford tractor and a 2 bottom plow from Vail and Ronnow Lee when I bought this farm but found I needed a team worse, so sold the tractor to Everest Hackett and bought a black French draft mare that weighed about 1400 pounds from my brother Clifford, and a brown half-breed Belgian horse from Chas. Mathews.

A wagon and mowing machine from Lafe Mathews' estate, a foot lift sulky plow from the Wm. Mathews estate, a new harness, [a] 3-section harrow and a potato planter and some small tools elsewhere and began farming, making carpenter work a winter and side line occupation. I was soon the largest grower of potatoes in Lincoln County, Nevada, and raised about 60 tons of first-class alfalfa hay each year, as well as some small grain and corn. These found a ready market for cash. I also had several dairy cows for a while but when it became unlawful to sell raw milk or cream or butter made from unpasturized cream, I sold all my cows but one. This one I sold for $300.00 and made a down payment on the home in St. George in April, 1951.

I sold my farm in Panaca to a Mr. Larry Neff in 1949 and rented a farm there the next two years. I had taken a small place in Caliente on my farm which I sold in 1951 and paid this on the St. George home, too. We tried to sell our home in Panaca in 1951, but no one would buy it, so we leased it and moved to St. George, anyway, on Thanksgiving day, 1951. The next spring we sold the home [in Panaca] to our renter, Ray Alger, for $3,000 and got $24,000 of it down, taking a second mortgage for the balance [of] $600. The $2,400 was paid on the St. George home, which more that half paid for it. Work was plentiful in St. George, and we sere paying from $100 to $200 per month on the home instead of the $33.75 agreed on until I fell from the top of the Arrowhead garage to the concrete floor below, a distance of about 14 feet, breaking my neck in the fall. For a wonder, I lived, and finished paying for the St. George home.

I have overlooked telling of some of the work I did while living at Panaca, in my haste to get this history finished. I helped build the mortuary and county hospital at Caliente, and helped build the balcony around the top of the first story of the Cornelius Hotel. Did most of the finishing work in the county hospital. Also built several new homes in the town as well as remodeling quite a few prominent ones. Among the latter was the home of Mayor Thos. Dixon. I built two new homes and remodeled several others, and helped build and did most of the finishing work in the addition to the Pioche Grammar School building, which was done under the N.Y.A. program.

Among the prominent new homes I built in Panaca was the home of Prof. Frank Wilcox, principal of Lincoln Co. High School, and the home of Prof. Jos. E. Theriot, head of the music department of the high school.[I] helped build and did most of the finishing work in the Panaca Ward chapel, and was supervisor of construction and did most of the carpenter work in transforming the old ward chapel into a stake store house and stake office. I also had charge of the construction of the metal working school here which was built under the N.Y.A. system.

As supervisor, it was required that I have a regular teachers certificate, as I would be [an] instructor in this work. So I was issued a temporary certificate to teach building construction. Prof. Wilcox was quite happy over this certificate as he had been trying for years to get me in the school as [an] instructor in wood work and agriculture, and thought he could get this temporary state teachers certificate made a permanent certificate so I could teach in the high school, but the state refused to do this on the grounds that I lacked two hours having enough college credits to qualify. I did some work in nearly every home in Panaca, and built 125 kitchen cabinets in Lincoln County while living there.

I also learned house wiring and plumbing from my son-in-law, Whitney A. Cude, who was a graduate of the Coyne School of Electricity of Chicago, Illinois, and did a lot of wiring and plumbing in Panaca and Caliente. I had helped Whitney get this training by guaranteeing his tuition and keeping Priscilla and the baby with us while he was going to school. He was so grateful for this help that he taught me wiring and plumbing as he worked on buildings for me after his return. He also gave me a lot of higher mathematics he learned at Coyne and at the Northwestern University of Chicago, and another school at Tacoma, Washington to which the government sent him for training before his entrance into the Navy as Fire Control, First Class, in the second world war.

I did considerable prospecting while living in Panaca, and still have [in 1957] four mine cabins in separate locations there, with good ore prospects at three of them; in fact, ore has been shipped from all of them.

To get back to St. George, I finished paying for my home here in October 1954 out of compensation awarded by the State Industrial Commission for my broken neck. But [I] could have paid it sooner if I hadn't got hurt. As I only got $110 per month from the state and could have made at least $300 per month if I could have kept well. Since coming back to St. George I have added a lot to the monuments I had here before. About 1924 Albert Miller and Joe Riding and I, with the help of a few others that I don't call to mind, put in a reinforcing six-inch concrete wall on the inside of the outside basement walls of the tabernacle to support the ends of the ceiling joists which were floor joists for the assembly room of the stake tabernacle.

The discovery of this condition was inspirational. Pres. Jos. K. Nicholes of the St. George stake passed notes to Albert Miller and I who were up in the balcony at stake conference, asking us to see that those up there didn't congregate in one place at the close of the meeting, but [that they] left quietly in single file, and saying he wanted to see us after the services. We requested that those up there file out quietly after the meeting, then went down to meet

Pres. Nicholes. Bro. Miller asked what the score was and he replied, "I don't know. I just felt impressed that something was wrong, and that if too many people got in one place the balcony might fall in."

We examined the pillars supporting the balcony and found them O.K. so went into the basement. Here we found that termites had eaten the door and window casing and frames away badly, leaving in places only the paint. We also found all the joists damaged by termites, and some of them eaten off on the ends. So we put in this concrete wall, then put in partitions and divided the north and sought sections into class rooms, the walls supporting the ceiling joists. Before this the joists were just supported by round timbers and the space left open for a dance floor, banquets and other recreations.

In the spring of 1952, Clarence Moss, acting as stake building supervisor, hired me to do the carpenter work necessary to install the pipe organ. With the help of Danny Hafen, I set up the studding on the balcony on each side in the west end, and put on rock lath to receive the plaster. After it was plastered, I reinforced and hung the doors and did the other finishing work, including the making and setting up [of] the grills. I also sound-proofed a room under the choir seats to house the blower and other mechanisms connected with the organ and covered the pipes to the sound chambers with plywood.

I finished this work Saturday afternoon and Clarence told me that night that he was out of work until he could get some plans approved, which might take a month. So I called Leon Jennings early Monday morning and he sent me right back to the tabernacle to do the carpenter work necessary to install the cooling system. I sawed five of the six holes for the cold air registers in the ceiling of the tabernacle and helped do all other work in connection with this improvement. I sawed the woodwork off one half-inch below the pendulum of the big clock in the belfry to make room for the water tank used in cooling the air.

This tank was so large it had to be cut up in sections with a torch, the pieces brought up through the window, set back in place and welded together again. So this tabernacle has a lot of my monuments.

Working for Clarence Moss, I helped finish Heber Thompson's home, put in partition studding, ceiling joists and roof on Dean Gardner's home, and helped finish it. Helped finish the Dixie Pioneer Memorial Hospital, setting a lot of the frames, hanging doors and casing openings, etc. Did all the finishing work in the lobby except the service window between the lobby and stock room, and helped put in nearly all the walks and retaining walls on the hospital grounds. Also, helped build the Church Cafe on the knoll west of St. George.

Working for Jennings, I helped build the Layton home in the SE part of St. George, helped make living apartments on the second floor of the Jennie Hall store building, helped finish their apartments south of their lumber yard, helped with remodeling for Bill McMullins's store and started to tear the roof off the old Arrowhead Garage, from which I fell, July 29, 1952, breaking my neck and injuring my left shoulder.

After that I had to confine myself to small jobs of remodeling and repair work mostly. Added on one room and did the remodeling for Cecil Lang at the Albert Lang home to make room for an old people's rest home. Did a lot of work on Emerald Cox's home. Closed in the balcony on the south and set posts under it. Made Lonore-type shutters for the windows and installed them. Put in some partitions and shelves in the basement. Lined three clothes closets with red cedar. Built two deck porches, built his car port west of the house, built a partition fence between his home and the neighbors lot. Built tool sheds and a play house, put the concrete mantel and shelves on his open air fireplace, as well as some other work.

Pole Roundy helped me with the car port and one tool house. Hung outside doors and windows in Maxine Brook's home and did a lot of other roof and other repair work, re-shingling, making and hanging screen doors, etc. Made quite a lot of furniture of native hard wood, and am now specializing in this work and repairing and refinishing furniture.

Suffered a heart attack, Feb. 21, 1956, and have been handicapped by this ever since. Had several light attacks between then and the last of October, 1956, when I had a severe one that put me in bed for a month. Had just got to feeling able to return to light work when I had another light attack Jan 20, 1957, from which I am now convalescing. This last one was possibly caused by mental and emotional strain and some lifting in connection with shipping children's clothing, which the West Elementary School had collected, and which Milton Moody and Vernon Worthen were kind enough to turn over to us for shipment to Whitney A. Cude for distribution to Korean orphans, in Korea, where he is stationed.

In this shipment was two dozen pairs of new stockings contributed by the Center Clothing Co., and one dozen pairs we bought. The shipment consisted of four boxes [of] clothing and two boxes [of] shoes.[Emphasis in original]

Part Two - Work

In writing about my early work, I have left out some history-making experiences that are also full of interest. So I recorded them here.

In my railroad work, I worked first at Beryl, Utah, when the old San Pedro, Los Angeles and Salt Lake railroad work started to build [the line] through from Milford, Utah to San Pedro, California. Hendrix Bros. of Deseret, Utah, had the contract and I went out there from [high] school in the early spring when I was about 16 years old and worked 10 hours a day. I stayed about ten days and by then had caught such a severe cold, caused I think, mainly by bad sleeping conditions, that I thought it wise to quit and go home. About 12 men slept in a railroad car with no ventilation unless a car door was left open.

The old heating stove would be filled with coal at night and the car heated up so warm you had to throw part of your covers off, then before morning it got so cold you didn't have enough cover to keep warm. No cots or mattresses, so about four men bought a bale of grass hay from the company, divided it into four [parts] and fluffed it up to sleep on. Nelson Terry, Johnny Alger and I walked to Enterprise from here in one day, about 30 miles through the brush, as there was no wagon road to follow.

About two years later Johnny Alger, Fritz Reber [?], High Roundy and I hauled all the ties on to the grade to build the railroad from Modena to Uvada. I drove one of Roundy's teams. That summer Jera Hunt, Elmer Hunt, Jacob Hunt and I hauled the timbers from Modena to the Ophir mine at State Line, Utah to build the Ophir Mill there. I was the oldest one of the crew, then 18, and some of the timbers were 36 feet long. This made it necessary to use our wagon gears without reaches [?], binding the point of the rear hounds [?] up to the timbers with one chain, and the short wagon-box reach [?] up to the timbers with another chain. Thus our loads were double bound.

It was also necessary to make a wide swing on turns in the road to avoid running the rear wheels off the road. Jake forgot about this once and run one hind wheel over a very large rock just below State Line and mashed a rear wheel down. This necessitated reloading his timbers on another wagon as none of the rest of us drove a Mitchell Wagon, and our wheels wouldn't work on his axle. We camped at the "Head Waters" in the canyon about midway between Modena and the mine, and turned our horses out to graze at night. We would drive to Modena and load up and back to camp one day and to the mine and back the next. Ted chopped corn and oats to supplement the grass.

The next spring I went with Johnny Alger out to Acoma, Nevada, between Modena, Utah and Caliente, Nevada, to work. It seems the Oregon Short Line had built the grade, but had failed to keep the taxes paid, so the A.W. Clark interests of Montana had bought the grade from Nevada for taxes. The Oregon Short Line had started to build through from Uvada to Caliente, Nevada, and Clark hired a crew of men and stationed them at Acoma, Nevada, to delay this construction work. I was on of this crew. The Short Line offered a bonus of $25.00 for every load of ties their men could get on to the railroad grade and it was our job to see that no team got on the grade with a load of ties.

The teamsters would load with ties and drive up on a ridge north of the grade then, headed south and west, would start their teams on a gallop toward the grade. Johnny Alger and I worked together and I would run with the left hand horse, grab hold of the harness and unsnap the outside check. Johnny would do the same on the other side, except that he would reach under the horses neck and unsnap the inside check or fork of the lines. Then we would get out of the way and leave the driver with only his right hand line attached to the horses bits, so he would turn the team away from the grade himself. A few wagons were toppled over, but no one was hurt, as the driver would jump onto one of his horses when his wagon tipped.

One day we were all kept in camp to prevent the railroad bridge gang from putting in a bridge across a side wash at Acoma. George A. Holt, Bishop of Hebron and Enterprise was our foreman, and a Mr. Lambert was foreman of the Bridge Gang. When the Bridge Gang came up to the wash, their foreman walked out in front and said he was foreman of the gang and hoped no one would get hurt. Uncle George (George A. Holt was my uncle) stepped out and said he was foreman of our crew and that he had instructed his men to just rassle [wrestle] and scuffle with Lambert's men and prevent them from the placing [of] any bridge timbers.

Then they recognized each other. They had been companions while serving as missionaries for the L.D.S. Church in the Southern States, years before. So after greeting each other, [Mr.] Lambert said, "Elder Holt, you said something about rassling [wrestling]. We used to rassle in the mission field. Seems it was about nip and tuck between us, so I tell you what lets do. I'll rassle you to see if we put in the bridge. If I throw you, we put in the bridge. If you throw me we won't try to put it in." So Uncle George agreed. Lambert selected a referee and Uncle George selected me for his referee. The referees measured the distance and made the ring, and the two foremen got in and took holds for side holt rassling.

At the word "go", they started to tussle and Uncle George threw Lambert. Lambert Got the next fall, but Holt got the third, thus winning the match. Lambert just turned to his men and said, "We keep our word, we will not build the bridge." Both crews stayed there and pitched horse shoes, run races, jumped, boxed hats [?] and rassled to pass away the time. Eventually I rassled Lambert's referee and threw him. Then Lambert said, "You see what happened. I was about to suggest that my referee rassle one of your men, but you would have won anyway." And Uncle George said, "Yes. This boy's father is champion side-holt [-hold] rassler of Southern Utah, and he has rassled a lot with his father. That's why he was my referee." Soon after this the Supreme Court handed down a decision in the case, giving the grade to the Short Line on condition they reimburse Clark for all expenses connected with the grade.

I went from here down in the canyon between Clovervalley and Caliente and drove a team for Tommy Terry and we repaired and rebuilt the grade to Caliente. When the railroad was built on through toward California from Modena, more water was required at Modena. Up to this time all the water in Modena came from two wells with windmills on them at the Lynch and Clark places, old stations on the stage road between Delamar and Milford. This water was piped to Modena, a mile away in a two inch pipe, and water was sold there to freighters at 25 cents, per team, 15 cents for single horses or cows, and 25 cents per 50-gallon barrel.

Now the railroad needed more water, so the company went up to the Lynch Meadow and excavated deep trenches and put in drain pipe to get an adequate supply of water. I worked a while on this water system, then was offered a job with B.J. Lund & Co. of Modena which I accepted and worked for them most of the time until the summer of 1903 when I was married. At this time the company were [railroad] forwarding agents, and also sold hay, grain and flour and run a livery and feed stable. They bought the store later. My job here was driving stage and freight teams, shoeing horses, selling hay, grain and flour, unloading coke and coal, receiving copper ore and copper bullion, and loading these into cars for railroad shipment when a car load of either accumulated. Setting up wagons and buggies that were shipped in by railroad in the knock down [condition], forwarding merchandise to stores that were served from Modena, etc. I sold a car load of flour here one morning before breakfast for cash, a lot of it gold coin.

[I] see I have left out some important buildings I worked on while living in St. George, so [I'll] record them here.

I put in the foundation for the power plant for the Dixie Power Co. at Gunlock, then was induced to quit and take over the cabinet shop for Pickett Lumber Co. but this proved to be a mistake, as I got my right hand in the joiner soon after starting to work here. I was laid up about a month because of the loss of the tips of three fingers. Picketts wouldn't keep their word with me over the loss of these fingers, so I quit, and after a while went to Zion's Park and helped remodel the hotel and build a lot of the cabins there. Lionel Chidester of Panguitch, who was my helper, and I did all the work in the men's rest rooms in the hotel or lodge, and did the finishing in a lot of the guest cabins.

Then I was transferred into the shop and did cabinet work for about six weeks. Here, I made the tables for the kitchen, a seat for the barber shop, key file case, quite a number of cabin doors, and nearly all the screen doors for the lodges and cabins. Also a lot of screen sash. After the lodge work was done, I helped put in the foundation for the large garage a mile below the lodge, then the crew was split and I was sent to Cedar Breaks as assistant foreman there. Hy Hunz was foreman. The first job assigned me here was finishing the roof on the lodge. The common rafters and hip rafters had been put on the fall before, but the carpenters couldn't cut the jack rafters. They were trying to cut them in a miter box, but this won't work on round timbers because of the difference in the taper of poles in the forest.

To frame round timbers in the [rough] one strikes a line down the center of the timber and lays off his angles, etc., on this line. No two will come out with the same angle if cut in a miter box. I was given Wesley Pearce as a helper and we put the jack rafters and sheeting on the lodge and Royal Gardens of Cedar City and I shingled it. Then with George Casen as my helper we put in the windows and hung the doors, and I built the cigar case and confectionery cases on the mezzanine floor. From the very beginning of the job I had been saving the best finishing lumber for this purpose, as I knew it was to be done, then when I got it finished and was all ready to be varnished, we got orders to veneer it with slabs!

About the most intricate and complicated roof I ever put on is on an ore bin at Deerlodge, [Nevada]. We found it too cold here to sort ore in the winter outside, so run the walls of the ore bin up to about a seven foot ceiling and I put a roof on it. The bin was six feet wide at one end and 20 feet wide at the other. Eighteen feet long on one side and 22 feet long on the other. I put a hip roof on this bin, and had to cut every common rafter and every jack rafter a different length and different angles. The rafters all fit and it is a good looking roof. I shingled it with cedar shingles.

One place I worked that I was overlooking was a stretch one spring at the iron mines in the vicinity of the present working at the Iron Mound. We were doing work to patent the mines. We went on a strike one day for a raise from $1.25 and board to $1.75 and board for an eight hour day. Mr. Lurch, foreman for Milner, Dear and Lurch granted the raise but fired every man that struck as soon as he could be replaced. My brother, Will, and I were fired for this reason.

Another experience I am overlooking is work I did for the Caliente Rapid Transfer Co. at Caliente, Nevada, and Carol Miller, their foreman. I went to work for them early one spring under C.A. Kelley as carpenter foreman. Kelley was a hard man to work for. We had a store building and some lumber sheds to build for the company and some apartments to put up for Mr. Miller. This store building had a complicated roof, too, as the building was wider at one end than the other and one side longer than the other, occasioned by building to property line on one side and square with Front St. on the other. Property lines run north and south but Front St. didn't run east and west, but bore to the south at about a 10 or 15 degree angle.

I believe I cut the rafters on one side of all the same length to hold the ridge level but had to cut each rafter on the other side a different length and pitch. The roof looked all right, though when it was finished. A Mr. Tracy, who was foreman for an Ely, Nevada company that had a contract on the highway from Pioche to

Caliente wanted me to go to work for them on highway bridges. I worked all night two nights for him, and in Caliente, [I still worked] day shift, but when he came for me the third time I refused, saying I couldn't work night and day. Then he offered me 25 cents per hour more than I was getting if I would come on for them steady. I was tired of Kelley's abuse, so told him if Kelly was still Miller's foreman when I went to work the next morning, I would quit and come on the bridges.

I had all the material for the drawers for the hardware store out, ready to put together, piled up on the bench at the north end of the store. I just drove into the yard the next morning in time to see Kelley pick up a short board and scrape all those drawer parts off on the ground and started to drag the bench off (The bench was his). I told him I would help him with it and asked where he wanted to take it. He motioned to his pickup near by. I helped him load it , then he got his tool box and saw-horses and put them on and I asked where he was going. He told me to watch him and see. Then he said Miller thought he could get along without him but he knew he couldn't, as there was no one else around there who could handle the job. [He] said that Miller would be after him to come back in a few days, then he would make him pay more to get him.

I gathered up the drawer material, and went to the lumber shed and started to get lumber to make another bench, when Mr. Miller came and asked me if I would mind leaving the store work a few days and go over and run the concrete crew that was pouring the foundations for the apartment buildings. He said he had canned Kelly, as he was sick and tired of his yowling. [He] said Kelley was knocking me all the time, but he had noticed that anything I did looked like an artisan had done it, but everything Kelley did looked like a farmer had made it. He told me I would be in charge of all the work from there out at a raise of 25 cents per hour.

I went over to the apartment builders and asked what Kelley did over there. My son-in-law, Whitney Cude, who was running the concrete mixer said he ran around and hollered and cussed, mostly. I said that Kelley had quit and Miller had sent me over to work in his place. One of the boys said, "Quit, my eye! Miller has been over here. He told us he fired Kelley and you would take his place as foreman, and we all welcome the change." They were ready to go so I said they knew what to do, and I would work on the forms and do the tamping and got a tamping iron and went to work. About ten o'clock, Miller came over and asked me what was the matter. I told him nothing was wrong so far as I knew. He said it was so quiet over there he thought maybe we had broke the mixer. The boys all laughed and said they liked it that quiet.

We poured ten bags more cement that day than the crew ever did under Kelley, and 20 bags more the next day and finished the job early. Whitney and I went back to the store the next day and I made a new work bench and began putting drawers together, and Whitney finished the electric work. Two days later we stripped the forms off the foundation and found the work done the last two days [to be] very much smoother and better than that done before. Whitney started roughing in the plumbing the next day and I cut studding on a power saw. I probably helped him with the plumbing, as we worked together; me helping him then he helping me.

When the plumbing was roughed in we put down the floor joists and laid the subfloor, then put up the walls and roof, roughed in the wiring and put on Celotex lath. When the building was ready for plaster, Whitney went on another wiring job and I spent a day or two at the store catching up the odd ends of finishing, then tore the kitchen cabinet out of Miller's new home and built a more modern one. Finishing these two four-room double apartments, 16 rooms, and building additional lumber sheds kept me busy until late in the fall.

I remember, too, we took time out from this work in August and lined the company's liquor store room with insulating Celotex block about two feet wide by three feet long and three inches thick. These were stuck on the wall with paste. This was a tough job, as the temperature outside was around 110ø and the inside kept to 40ø with cooling apparatus. The paste had to be put on outside where it was warm or it wouldn't stick, so we took turns [, one of us] putting on paste and [the other] sticking blocks. From 110ø to 40ø is a big change in temperature, and it seemed greater when one changed the other way.

The Caliente Rapid Transfer Co., did freighting by truck, ran a lumber yard, sold coal, ran a hardware store, and were wholesale liquor dealers, etc. My daughter kept books for them while home from school on vacation [for] one or two years. My policy and that of C. A. Kelley in relation to building were exactly opposites. I tried to hold the cost of building down while Kelley believed in keeping the cost as high as possible. In building forms for foundations I sawed 2x4 studding the right length to use a 2x4 plate top and bottom and put the forms together in sections on the ground then set them in place. These short 2x4 studding could be cut again and used as short studs over and under openings, as headers and fire wall with little or no waste, while Kelley drove stakes made of first grade flooring or 1x4 pine finishing lumber in the ground to a line on both sides of the foundation. Then starting at the right height for the top of the foundation nailed lumber on the inside of these stakes to make his forms.

The first side could be nailed on quite fast, but the other side, in an eight-inch space, was slow nailing. Then he put a 2x4 flat against the stakes on the outside at the top of the wall and tied the forms together with heavy wire. This also was slow and expensive. Then when the forms were stripped, these stakes made of high priced lumber were just burned up. If he wasn't watched, he would haul off short pieces of finishing lumber I had cut for special places and burn them in his cook stove at home. We just couldn't work together.

I built a pulpit in the Protestant Church in Caliente at the invitation of Percy Moore, manager of J.C. Penny Company's store there. He was a member or chairman of a committee of the church which had the responsibility of this sort of improvement. When it was done, I refused payment for it, saying I always did that sort of thing gratis. He said he could understand why I should do it [for] free for my own church, but couldn't see why I should do the same thing for his church. I told him I had no quarrel with any church or its members over our religious differences, because if his church was wrong it wasn't his fault, he didn't organize it or fix its doctrines, and if mine was wrong it wasn't my fault for the same reasons.

I saw a palimpsest [look it up!] at Caliente. It was shown [to] me by a Catholic Priest. The underwriting, which was plainly visible with a high power reading glass was, he said, written in Hebrew, and as he had translated it, it gave an account of the prophet Jared and his brother, Mahonri Moriancumer, who led a colony from the tower of Babel, possibly to this continent under the direction of God and established a great civilization in North America that lasted for 1600 years. This would account for a lot of the very old signs of civilization that have been discovered in North America, especially in Mexico. (After "Tower of Babel" is my interpretation.)

I have mentioned working on the Enterprise reservoirs and canals, but their is some of this that I think I should tell a little more in detail.

I helped put in the first undercurrent dam at the mouth of Cow Hollow at the old Huntsman ranch and the canal from this dam. These were tough and slow propositions with the little equipment we had then. One might say no equipment. We bought lumber and nailed cleats on inch [thick] boards, about ten inches wide to make a section 30 inches wide and about 14 feet long. The ends were about three feet wide . One of these sections was set in place and men and boys would get inside it and shovel sand and dip water out and settle it a little more than its depth in the sand then another section was set on top of it and cleated to it and then two forms settled as deep as possible, usually about five feet. Then clay was hauled in with teams and the forms filled with clay.

When this one was filled another one was settled the same way. When there were workers enough while one crew was hauling clay, another crew was setting and settling forms in the sand, end to end. But it took six men and boys to settle a form and about six to a team hauling clay as the clay had to be loaded and unloaded by hand with shovels. But by doing this we cut off the water that was running in the sand and brought it out into our canal. This was the first water brought into Enterprise. And to make the canal was no easier. The wash bank at the head of the canal was ten or twelve feet high and this bank had to be worked down for the canal as the sand was right up to the bank. We cut it down a little way with shovels, then when we got a shelf wide enough for a team we put teams on with plows and plowed the bank down, and this had to be done for a distance of about half a mile before we could gain grade enough to get on top of the ground. It took us months to do what could be done now with a bulldozer in a few hours. We got about three second-feet of water out of the wash by this method. I later baptized my nephew and niece, Herbert and Helen Hackett, in this canal a few years later. These were children of my sister Sarah [Hall] and Everest Hackett of Deerlodge, Nevada.

I also worked on both of the Enterprise reservoirs. The first or big one was a slow job too. There was twelve feet of solid masonry on the lower side, built in a curve with the bulge up stream. The rock for this had to be hauled quite a distance from the quarry, and the lime of which the mortar was made was hauled from the kiln about three miles southeast of Enterprise in Cottonwood Canyon. I helped burn some of this lime and hauled some of it to the reservoir. Above this masonry wall was 100 feet of earth fill, and a six foot riprap wall against the water. The dirt was hauled in with teams in a special wagon box with a loose bottom of 2x6 planks with each end worked down edgewise to about three inches wide to allow a man to take hold of each one separately and turn them up on edge to let the dirt out.

Two men were on hand all the time to do this, one working at each end of the wagon. The teamster would drive to an indicated place on the dam and be unloaded in this way, then go for another load of dirt. And the wagons were loaded for a long time with shovels, then a regular loading pit was made and the wagons loaded by teams pulling dirt up with tongue scrapers and dumping it into the wagons through a grid. The riprapping was done by men who understood this sort of thing, which required quite large flat stones, laid to resemble the scales on a fish. The masonry wall was perpendicular on the outside, but tapered back against the dirt to about 6 feet in thickness at the top. The small reservoir, which was built later, is just a solid concrete wall reinforced with steel and built in a curve across the channel from cliff to cliff. I was flagman for the engineer when this was surveyed, and helped put in the forms for the foundation, with short steel rods in this to which long rods were tied when the main wall was poured. I also helped survey the overflow from this reservoir, which was cut through the ridge between the two reservoirs where the overflow from this one ran into the big reservoir. The most of the living water was below the big reservoir, which was the reason for building the little one.

While traveling [later] for the Utah Woolen Mills, I had a new car robe stolen out of my car. It showed up a week or so later in a car whose owner said his son found it. when I said I lost one like it, he put it in my car saying he didn't want [it]. I asked where the boy was and he told me he was working at the tunnel camp in Zion Park. I went to the park and phoned the boy to meet me on the trail. When we met I failed, at first, to talk him into the truth about the robe. I started back down to my car then thought, "has scouting failed?"

The boy was in my troop a few years before and had passed Tenderfoot and Second Class with me. So I turned back and called him. He stopped and I went and put my arm around him and said "I, too, have sinned". He looked across the canyon at the massive cliffs and began to cry. Then he told me he took the robe out of my car while I was in the picture show. He named a few quite prominent men who were hiring him to "lift" articles from tourists cars at a dollar each. After taking this robe he noticed it was my car but I came out of the show before he could get to it. He refused the dollar promised for it and kept the robe. After an almost sleepless night he decided to leave town and go off to work to get away from these men, so he could reform. He had met a lovely girl whom he could never face with this guilt on his conscience.

Years later, when living at Panaca, Nevada, I was out on a little-traveled road, [looking for] posts. I had scratched my hands, one cheek, which was smeared with blood, and torn my shirt. While eating lunch by my pickup a car passed by then immediately stopped. A man came back. It was that boy! He put his arms around me and kissed me on the blood stained cheek and told me I would never know what I did for him. He had married that lovely girl and they had three children. He had told her all about the robe. I went to the car with him and the "lovely girl" kissed me on the same cheek. Compensation! Compensation!

Part Three – Music

My first study of music was under my father W[illiam] W[esley] Hall, who was a top student of Betty Butler, a Welsh-trained chorister and music teacher, who joined the church in Wales, emigrated to the US and settled in Escalante [,Utah]. Under my fathers teaching I was playing a violin by note at 10 years of age, playing in a dance orchestra at 12, and at 14 was playing lead violin in a dance orchestra. My father also held a music school each winter which I attended at 13 and 14 years of age. In this school we were taught to read music, the principle of time, and how to beat it with the baton, and how to do conducting. He used the "Sol-Fa" system, also teaching us how to get the proper pitch of any key by using a 'C' tuning fork.

When I was 14 years old I was sustained as chorister of the first Sunday school and also of the first Primary organization in Enterprise [Utah]. I served as Sunday school chorister nearly all the time I lived there and part of the time as assistant ward chorister. I also played 1st violin, first cornet, guitar, five-string banjo, cello and [during] the last year I was there, an E-flat clarinet in the dance orchestra.

When I was about 16 years old I worked in State Line, Utah, [a now-extinct town near the town of Hamblin Valley] and played both guitar and violin in the dance orchestra there. The members [of the band] were Amos W. Hall, violin or guitar; Job F. Hall, same; Will Schoppman, organ or violin; Billy Presnell, organ or guitar; Ed. W. Hall, mandolin and official square-dance caller; Reginald (Reggy) Pepper, concertina; and Paul Poyner, clarinet. All these men have passed on now, except my brother Ed and I, unless Paul Poyner is still alive. The last time I heard from him he was playing E-flat clarinet in [John Phillips] Sousa's band in Chicago, Ill. I taught Will Schoppman to play the violin when I was going to school to his father in Hebron [,Utah]. I was about 14 years old at the time. While working at State Line I served as Sunday school chorister there.

When I was stake chairman of genealogy in the Uvada Stake, we got orders to send into the Church Genealogical Society at Salt Lake, a list of all the people who were buried in our stake. There were about twenty ghost towns in the Uvada Stake, with from 1 to 3 cemeteries at each [one]. So the stake committee told the ward committees that if they would list their ward cemeteries, we would do the ghost towns. Under this agreement Delamar, Bullionville, Fay, Deerlodge and Atlanta fell to me.

I drove to Atlanta, 87 miles from Panaca [, Nevada], and found that only one person had been buried there, and to my surprise it was this Reginald Pepper who played the concertina in our orchestra at State Line about 50 years before. He was born in Cornwall, England.

I note that I said [earlier that] my father used the "Sol-Fa" system . I think it is the best system for teaching vocal music. By this system one gets the tones of the scale fixed in their minds. Do-rey-mi-fa-sol-la-ti-do, is much more comprehensive than C-D-E-F-G-A-B-C or G-A-B-C-D-E-F#-G. Do-rey-mi-fa-sol-la-ti-do is used in every key, beginning with 'do' on the key note. To get the pitch of a key with a C-tuning fork, if the key is sharps, one calls the pitch of the fork 'do' and runs up to 'sol', and calls that tone 'do'. This would be the key note, or G, if the piece was in the key of G. If the piece was in the key of D, two sharps, one would run up to 'sol' again and call that 'do'. This would be the key note or 'do' for the key of D.

If the key was in flats, one starts the same way but runs up do-rey-me-fa and calls 'fa', 'do'; this would be F or one flat. If two flats were used as the key signature then calling this 'fa', 'do', run down, do-ti-la-sol-fa, and call this 'do'. That would be B-flat, etc., running to 'sol' as many times as there were sharps in the key signature, and to 'fa' as many times as there were flats in the signature, calling 'sol', 'do', and 'fa', 'do' each time as the case may be. [Hence the name, Sol-fa.]

I conducted the Sunday school and ward choir at Enterprise and at Hatch [,Utah] when neither place had an organ and used this method to get the pitch of the key the song was in, in both towns.

When I was 16 years old my brother Amos and I joined R. M. Rogers, a Photographer who came to Enterprise and spent about three months with him. I wanted to learn the business, and Amos went along to get feed for his team and his board. He served as cook and dish washer for us to pay for these things, and made a little money on the side teaching violin and playing for dances. We went first to Pinto[, Utah] where we stayed about six weeks. While here I served as Sunday school chorister and played violin and guitar in the dance orchestra.

After getting all the [photo] business we could in Pinto, we moved on to New Harmony[, Utah] where the same procedure was carried out. I served as Sunday school chorister and played in the dance orchestra. Just before we finished at New Harmony, my father and Jas. E. [Jim] Hall (no relation) came to [New] Harmony to finish their little church and do other carpenter work. I found Rogers hard to get along with by now, so quit and helped my father and Jim in their carpenter work. We finished the church, put in shelves and counters in Bishop Red's store and built a barn for Sarah Prince. I gave her son, Antone Prince, violin lessons while working here.

I learned the photo business well enough to do this type of work for myself and have a lot of pictures I took with a small camera I bought and printed, finished and mounted the pictures myself.

On our return to Enterprise, I took over the Sunday school chorister job again and played violin in dances. About this time I learned to play a fife and played in a martial band (Fife & Drum Corps). I continued my music work here quite steadily until I was about 20 years old. By then my sister, Mary, had married Johnny Alger, a close friend of mine who had played guitar a lot with me in dances. They had gone to Hatch with Johnny's father, and persuaded me to go with them. While there I helped build his father's home and served again as Sunday school chorister, and played violin in the dance orchestra.

Here I met Annie Clove, Johnny's cousin whom I later married in the St. George temple, and who has been a wonderful wife and mother of our children. We lived in Hatch several years after our marriage, built a store there, and I went on a mission from there. All the while we lived at Hatch, I served as Sunday school chorister and played for their dances. I also served as assistant ward chorister and ward chorister.

While living here I took another chorister's course under Wm. T. Owens, another Welsh-trained chorister who joined the church in Wales and came over and settled in Panguitch[, Utah]. He was Panguitch Stake chorister and ruled that all ward choristers belonged to the stake choir and asked them to take a chorister's course he was giving in Panguitch. The stake paid the tuition and the choristers their own transportation. Roy Porter, my assistant, and I took the course, going horseback some times and some times by team. Owens was an excellent chorister and teacher.

I left Hatch because of my health in 1907 and in 1908 went to Beaver[, Utah] to school at the Murdock Academy, then a branch of the B.Y.U. at Provo. Here I majored in music and mathematics, studying harmony and composition and conducting under Prof. Geo. Durham and counterpoint and thorough [?] bass, and time and rhythm under Prof. Geo. Woodhouse. Also took band and orchestra under Woodhouse. Played violin in the orchestra and learned to play cornet, alto, baritone, and tenor horns. I just substituted on the last three when the regular performer was absent. Otherwise, I played 2nd B-flat cornet.

Soon after enrolling at the Murdock Academy, I had a conference with Josiah E. Hickman, Principal. At this conference it was agreed that I was to succeed John L. McQuarrie as head of the Woodwork Dept. in the fall of 1909, on his salary, and to assist Prof. Durham in the music dept., for tuition for my wife and I, and in the fall of 1910 was to take Prof. Geo. H. Durham's place as head of the music dept., as Bro. Durham wanted to leave and join the music staff at the McCune school of Music, and I was to teach that same year in the math dept.

But I went to work on the opera house under construction in Beaver to earn a little money during the Christmas Holidays to supplement my finances. But I got so seriously injured the second day that I was laid up at school under the care of Dr. Donald McGregor for a month. At the end of the month I was still unable to attend classes so Dr. McGregor advised me to go home where I could rest and gain my health again.

I did this, intending to teach and go to school, as I had arranged to finish the music and math courses by correspondence. But Will Lund wrote me soon after returning home and offered me a job in the store in Modena[, Utah]. So I accepted the offer and went to Modena the last of March and had become so interested in business that I stayed there instead of returning to school. Had it not been for that accident, in which I saved a man's life, I would no doubt have been a school teacher.

A branch Sunday school was organized in Modena and I was chorister. The fall [of 1910 that my daughter] Grace was born I quit the store in Modena and returned to Enterprise and served again as Sunday school chorister. Part of the next few years we lived on our dry-farm at the Point of Rocks. While living here we would load our organ into a white-top buggy, occasionally, and take it over to the Newcastle Hotel and play for a dance, Annie playing the organ and I the violin. We absented ourselves from the farm two different years and went to Lund where I worked as clerk and bookkeeper for H. J. Doolittle Co. While here I was chorister of a small Sunday school and played for the dances.

In the fall of 1914 we went to Escalante where I had a chance to buy an interest in my brother, Amos', store. I was sustained as M.I.A. chorister here and had charge of all M.I.A. music activities. I organized a male quartet, [a] ladies quartet, and a double mixed chorus. My groups won first place that winter in the Panguitch Stake music contest, conducted by the stake M.I.A. I also played first violin in a concert orchestra while here, and took part in other music activities and was comedian in the Mutual plays. I did a lot of this kind of work in every ward in which I lived, usually playing character parts; Negro, Irish, Dutch, English Piccadilly, and others.

I found the store in Escalante too small to justify a two-man ownership, so returned to Enterprise. I was always a part of the musical and theatrical life of Enterprise, as well as all other towns in which I lived any length of time. While living in the Enterprise Ward [on my farm] at Point-of-Rocks and [later at] Hebron, I rode horseback many nights five and six miles into Enterprise for choir practice and rehearsal for plays.

In the spring of 1921 we traded our ranch at Hebron for part of the Bastian Farm near Washington[, Utah] and moved down there. Almost immediately I was sustained as ward Sunday school and

M.I.A. chorister and [played] violinist in the dance orchestra. I was also selected as dramatic coach for M.I.A. and coached and took part in all the plays put on there for two years. In the fall of 1923 we sold out in Washington and went to St. George[, Utah]. The second Sunday I was in St. George, I was sustained as Sunday school chorister in the West Ward. The next spring we rented a home for a while in the East Ward and I served as Sunday school chorister in the East Ward . Then I bought the old Walter Dodge home in the West Ward and was sustained again as chorister of the ward, Sunday school and M.I.A. I continued in these positions all the time I lived in the West Ward. While living in St. George, I attended the Dixie College a few winters and took the full college course in music under Jos. W. McAllister. Just before coming to St. George from Washington, I sat by the tabernacle and listened to the stake choir practicing for conference and wondered if I would ever sing in that choir. I [,later,] not only sang in it but conducted it while living in St. George, as I served the last two years I lived here as assistant stake chorister.

After we had been here a few years and [our daughters,] Grace and Priscilla got older we sang soprano, alto and baritone trios together, singing on programs at Dixie College and in all three wards in St. George and other wards in the surrounding towns. I also had a Hill-Billy type orchestra consisting of Job Hall, violin; Bob Kenworthy, piano accordion; Art Kemp, Octophone; Vere Whipple, banjo; and Harry Fullerton, guitar. We did a lot of program playing for various organizations, both religious and civic in St. George and a few dances elsewhere, but couldn't get to play for dances in St. George as the college kept all dance halls hired and the ones they couldn't use locked up to protect school orchestras. I did a lot of singing solos here and in various wards, in sacrament meetings, Mutuals, funerals, etc., as well as in civic organizations.

The last four or five years I lived here I traveled part-time for the Utah Woolen Mills and other clothing firms selling direct. In my travels, I have acted as Sunday school or ward chorister, in Paragonah, Glendale, Orderville, Springdale, Rockville, Kanab [,all Utah], Fredonia[, Arizona], Mesquite, Bunkerville, Logandale, Overton, Las Vegas, Elgin, Caliente, Panaca, Barclay, Pioche and Bristol Silver [all Nevada], and probably a few other towns.

I have mentioned playing guitar in orchestras. Well, in May 1933, I was stricken with a severe illness, so, while convalescing, I went to work on the guitar in earnest, as I could play it lying on my back in bed. I figured out new ways of tuning a guitar so I could play melodies and accompaniment on it similar to the piano method. After that, I played guitar solos, and sang with the guitar on many sacred and civic programs. I spent Christmas of 1933 in Salt Lake City and played in Christiansen Music Co.'s store and in Beesley's in Salt Lake. I also broadcast over [radio station] K.S.L. at the suggestion of Fred A. Beesley of Beesley Music Co., who got me an audition with Mr. Southworth, manager of K.S.L. at that time.

I played on the "Utah Buckeroos" program and it went over so good that Mr. Southworth called [my daughter] Priscilla's home [in Salt Lake] after I had left Salt Lake City and wanted me to come and do some more broadcasting. I played on the buckeroos program that summer when they were in St. George and promised to join them that fall in Salt Lake City, but got too much interested in mining in Deer Lodge, Nevada, to go.

While in Salt Lake during the Christmas holidays, Fred A. Beesley wanted me to write some books on my method of playing the guitar. He offered to fix me up a studio in their store where I could teach guitar and to turn their guitar department [in the store] over to me and pay me a commission on all guitars I sold, and in my spare time I was to write these books. He would pay all expenses of music paper, printing binding and copywriting the books for ten percent royalty on the sales. This is probably where I missed an opportunity.

Once, after this , Prof. Jos. E. Theriot, head of vocal music at Lincoln County High school in Panaca, Nevada, offered me several reams of music paper at ten percent of cost, if I would write some instructions on my method of playing guitar. I figured I was just too busy and too much involved financially to do it. I had bought a farm and had to spend most of my winters building houses and marketing my potatoes to pay for the farm.

While in Panaca, I took two more Conductors for Choristers courses. One under Eldon Larson of Las Vegas[, Nevada] and one under N. Lorenzo Mitchell of the church music committee who lives in Salt Lake City. I also sang in the Panaca Ward choir with Wayne Kirk as conductor. This experience was equal to another chorister course, as Bro. Kirk, who came from Tooele, Utah was recognized as one of the best choral conductors in the church. The Combined Metals Production Co. had brought him in for special work in their mill at Castleton. I was ward clerk at the time and visited every new member and got a line on their abilities. After talking with

Bro. Kirk, I convinced Earl Long, ward chorister, to resign in Bro. Kirk's favor. Bro. Long w s very cooperative. I was his assistant.

I had gone to Deer Lodge, Nevada, in early spring of 1934 to work with my brother-in-law, Everest Hackett in the mines there. While there I taught his daughter, Mary, to play guitar by my method. She became very good on the guitar.

In the summer of 1935 I moved to Panaca, Nevada, and the second Sunday I was there, I was sustained [as] Sunday school Chorister, which position I held most of the sixteen years I lived there. I also served a lot of the time as ward chorister and Mutual chorister. I also played violin in one dance orchestra, and guitar or piano in another. Did a lot of singing in quartets , duets, choruses, as well as quite a lot of solos in the area.

I have overlooked one experience in music that I believe is important. When I carried the mail from State Line[, Utah] to Pioche[, Nevada] just after we were married, I played in a dance orchestra at Pioche. This was a Star Mail route, and I rode a horse to Pioche one day and back to State Line the next. The first time I played in Pioche, I carried my violin tied on the saddle behind me. After this I left my violin in my room in Pioche so we could hold orchestra practice during the week. The orchestra consisted of violin, Job F. Hall; Cornet, Charley Thompson; Tenor horn, Roy Orr; Baritone or slide trombone, Al Carmen; piano, Wilkes Campbell and Charley Osborn.

In the fall of 1951, I returned to St. George, where I was immediately drafted into a dance orchestra, Hillbilly style, with Ted Liston, with whom I played some at Panaca; on violin, guitar or piano, Job F. Hall and Henry Graff; musical saw, Mr. Cook.

Later, I organized a Hillbilly style orchestra consisting of Job F. Hall, violin; Mrs. Baker, piano accordion; Lloyd Baker, tenor banjo; N. B. Roundy, mandolin; Raymond Laub, musical saw and [blank space] guitar. We were just ready to begin playing for dances and other public functions when I suffered a heart attack.

[Editor's Note: The following is taken from a letter dated April 16, 1957, written by Job from St. George to his daughter, Desma, in Salt Lake City who was collecting her father's stories for typing. fr]

Dear Desma,

Think it a good idea to add the following to my History, Music Dept. - viz.

I taught the following songs before they were ever published in any of our song books. They came out first in the Juvenile Instructor and in sheet music form, and I taught the songs from one of these sources.

Carry On
If There's Sunshine In Your Heart
Master the Tempest
Oh How Lovely Was The Morning
School Thy Feelings
Shall the Youth of Zion Falter?
True to the Faith

and possibly others.

Sometimes we either put on a play or gave a dance to raise money to buy sufficient copies of the sheet music for the Sunday school in which case I either directed the play or took a leading part in it, especially if there was a character part and sometimes did both, or if it was a dance I played in the dance orchestra, and all of us contributed our services.

[A footnote to this part of his history must include an incident that happened not to long after this. Job was visiting the family of his daughter, Grace, in California, and played his style of guitar and sang to his accompaniment. We had an early form of recorder, using steel wire instead of magnetic tape which we used to record Grandpa Hall playing for us. One day one of the children, home alone after school decided to play "disc jockey" and recorded over all of Grandpa's singing. I was that kid! I dearly wish, now, that I could somehow undo that damage so we could have an example of his playing. gfr]

Part Four – Scouting

My first experience in scouting was in the Washington [,Utah] Ward. I was sustained and registered as Scoutmaster when Mutual opened then in the early fall of 1921. I continued in this work until October, 1956, having spent 35 consecutive years in scouting. The only thing I have to show for it is my first Scoutmaster's badge that I bought in 1921 in Washington. I was given a 25 year pin when I had served 30 years but have lost it.

When I started to serve as Scoutmaster in Washington, I went in on an equal basis with the scouts. I knew nothing about it, but liked the boys. I had them studying Tenderfoot, 2nd Class and 1st Class work all at the same time instead of taking each rank in order. My salvation was a scout leadership course given that winter at the Dixie College. I believe it was at the course that I first met the wonderful scouter, Oscar A. Kirkham. I learned something of how to handle a scout troop at this leadership course, so soon had my troop properly organized into patrols, and all of them working on Tenderfoot requirements. I kept pace with them by studying a few pages ahead of them all the time. I had spent a lot of my time in the open, had done a lot of camping and had always been very observant of trees, shrubbery, earth formations, tracks and habits of birds, animals and reptiles. These things now became very useful to me. I could tell time of night and get my directions by the stars, and knew a lot of other things about nature that scouters need to know.

Early the next spring, we went on an overnight hike up on the Cottonwood Ditch. Each of us carried a quilt or a blanket, and food enough for four meals. We also carried a few cooking utensils. We ate lunch somewhere along the way and made camp at night up on the ridge where the cottonwood ditch came up from the spring. Here my observation of [animal] tracks paid off. I had told the boys at the campfire that night in the course of my remarks to them on tracking, that I could tell a rattlesnake track from other reptiles and could tell the direction he was going.

The next morning when we were getting ready to start back toward home, some of the boys were walking along near the ditch looking for fish, when they suddenly stopped and called [to] me. I went over where they were and they showed me the track of a snake and challenged me to tell if it was a rattler and which way he had gone. I examined the track and said that it was a rattlesnake and indicated the way it was going. As the track was fresh we followed it and came up with the snake about 25 or 30 yards farther on. It was a large one and showed fight immediately. But it didn't take us long to put it out of circulation. It had 10 rattles, as I remember it. A full account of this trip was published in the Washington County News of about May 1922.

At this period of scouting, a lot of attention was given to patrol and troop drill formation. I tried all the winter and spring to get my troop to go through some of these maneuvers, but to no avail.

When July 1922 came around, we decided to go to the big Scout Jamboree held at Pinevalley. As I remember it, brothers Oliver Belnap and Jos. Jolley took their teams and transported us to Pinevalley. The first night out we camped on the Cottonwood ditch, and had just got through with supper and were getting ready to make beds on the ground when it started to rain, and rained nearly all night, so we just huddled in the wagons under the wagon cover and got almost no sleep. By morning it had quit, but soon after we got on our way it began raining again and rained intermittently all day. That night we were assigned an old deserted home as our quarters. The house had been swept out and looked quite clean and comfortable so we got supper and made our beds and went to bed early, anticipating a good night's rest, but we had just been sleeping a short while when it started to rain again and the roof leaked, most places, just a little but some places quite bad. So some of the boys had to get up and move beds, but some just laid and took it.

The next day it cleared and we had good weather the balance of the trip. There were some scout activities held beginning at 10 o'clock, a.m. and some more that afternoon. At 7:00 o'clock p.m. the big night session was held. Each troop was assigned a certain position and were to march to this location and form a hollow square. The first few troops that marched to location did a nice job of it as they had been trained, but my troop was just a mob. I was very much embarrassed, but didn't say a word. My boys notice the difference too, and appreciated the fact that I made no comment.

We made the regular hike the next day to the top of Pinevalley Mountain, and looked down into the rough breaks on the south side. On our way back, Ranger Mit Moody showed us where the Douglas

Firs were cut that were taken to Salt Lake [City] and used to make pipes for the pipe organ in the Salt Lake Tabernacle.

The Jamboree was closed that night with a free dance and as we wanted to get an early start for home the next morning my scouts all agreed before we went to the dance that when I blew a certain signal on the scout whistle, they would all come and go to bed. When I blew the signal all the boys came but one. I asked where he was and two of the boys said he was with a girl in the shadow of a building near the dance hall, but refused to come with them. I went back but he refused to come with me so I just picked him up and put him on my shoulder and carried him to camp. He said he would go back, but two husky scouts took him in bed between them and he had to stay. He soon ceased to struggle, however, and went to sleep.

This boy thanked me years after for saving him from himself, saying he would likely have been a father at 15 if I hadn't rescued him. His father was angry at first, and said a boy should be allowed to live his own life. I replied that when a boy went with his troop to a scout camp he lived a scouts life.

The troop's embarrassment over the [poor] marching on this trip soon paid off for the very next evening after our return, [I was home when] I heard a crowd yelling and went outside to see what it was, and it was a lot of fellows swooping in on my place [on] horse back. I was living on the Bastion farm east of Washington. When they drew closer, I could see it was my scout troop and that each boy was carrying either a grubbing hoe, axe, rake or pitchfork. When they drew up I asked what it was all about and they said they wanted to clear a place drill.

I said we could clear a place right there across the wash north of my house, but they said it was too far away [from town] and that they had talked with Bishop Cal Hale about it and he told them they could have the use of some ground of his near town, and that if he should sell it at anytime he would pay them troop for clearing it. [They wanted me to go with them but] It was then nearly sundown and I had irrigated all day and wanted to wait until tomorrow, but they wanted to go right then, so I got my grubbing hoe and went with them. We cleared a splendid drill ground, but I didn't get to bed until two a.m.

The next day, I contacted Chester Thayne, a Drill Sergeant of World War I and secured his services as Drill Sergeant for the troop. Then we drilled nearly every night until I had the best trained troop in the whole area. Chester drilled the troop until I learned the different formations and calls for them then I acted as Drill Master. The next year at Pinevalley, my troop took 1st place instead of being the "Awkward Squad". From here on my troop made rapid progress. I served as scoutmaster here until the fall of 1923, when I moved to St. George and became affiliated with B. Jarvis Jr. in his troop. I had some good scouts at Washington, and some of them are prominent men in their communities. Preston Larso of Hurricane, Glen Tobler of Las Vegas, Clark Nisson of Henderson, Nevada, Woodrow Staheli [(?)] , bishop of Washington a year or so ago. Archie and Ernie Tobler, Tommy Nisson, Wayne Sandbury and others.

On May 11th, 1922, the Washington Co. News had this to say, "Scoutmaster Job F. Hall of Washington was a city visitor Wednesday. He reports the boys of that place [are] very enthusiastic about scout work. Nearly all of his boys have passed their tenderfoot work and are going along with the second class work."

I became very deeply engaged in scouting with Bro. Jarvis in the East Ward in St. George. Brother Jarvis had a very large troop and was glad to get some experienced help.

In July of 1924 we began to make preparations to go on a trip around Washington, Iron, Garfield and Kane counties to give the boys a chance to get acquainted with the area. We got a scout play " The Country Boy Scout", and began rehearsing it. We also fixed up two trucks especially for the trip, with the sides extended like a sheep wagon, food lockers on the sides and the truck wide enough to make beds crosswise on it.

We left on this trip, as reported in the Washington Co. News, on Wednesday, Aug. 20th 1924 and put on our play that night in Veyo. Many people from Gunlock and Central and other nearby places attended, the article says. We played at Enterprise Aug. 21st; Cedar City Aug. 23rd; Parowan Aug. 25th; and at Orderville, Aug. 30th. We wanted to put the play on in Panquitch but found their theatre bldg. engaged, so we went on to Panguitch Lake.

There were 30 boys and 3 scout leaders on this trip, a total of 33. It took 2 trucks and 3 touring cars to carry the party. My responsibility was to see that the larder was supplied. As few stores carried bread at that time, you would see start out canvassing a town for bread as soon as we stopped to make camp. The people were very generous, and most of them refused to accept money for bread. Milk, fruit and vegetables were also contributed in many places.

One woman, Mrs. Blackburn of Orderville, furnished bread free for the troop there. She also gave us the run of her apple orchard. My Aunt Sarah Foote, gave us a no. 3 tub full of ripe tomatoes. At a dairy on Panguitch Creek, we waited for them to milk in the evening and bought 10 gals of milk so we could have bread and milk for supper. We sat the 5 gal. cans in a cold spring where we camped and the milk was soon cold.

While waiting for the milk some of the boys started fishing in the creek, so just to make a laugh, I picked a little blue flower and told one of the boys if he would let me have his tackle I would show him how to fish. The boy handed his pole over and I took the grasshopper he had for bait off the hook and put the blue flower on. I cast the hook out into the creek and almost immediately had a strike. It was so hard [to pull in] I thought a piece of driftwood had caught on my hook. But I pulled and to my surprise had a 6 pound trout.

The wind blew so hard the next day that it was unsafe to go out on Panguitch Lake in boats to fish, so part of us went down the creek below the lake. We had wood grubs, angleworms and grasshoppers for bait but didn't catch many fish, and they were small. In desperation, I tried a blue flower again and caught the largest fish that was taken that day so all the boys started [to] use blue flowers and took quite a lot of fish. So we had a good mess for dinner.

According to the report of the troop in the County News, we went next to Bryce Canyon. Here we met Tom Mix, a noted movie star of the time who was there with a party making the picture, "The Deadwood Coach". Mix was a very nice fellow. Our troop furnished the music for a dance for his party at Syrett's Inn, at Bryce Canyon. I have forgotten just what instruments we had and who played, but I had my violin along, and I know Lenzie Sullivan played piano. Theron Thompson had a cornet and there were a few harmonicas and guitars in the troop.

From here we went to Orderville and made our last appearance with our play. The people at Hatch begged us to stay and play there, promising us a full house, but we had booked Orderville in advance and had no way of contacting them to change the date. In fact, we needed to get back home, as brother Jarvis, John McAllister and I had all left jobs to make the trip, our play had failed to pay expenses and we were nearly broke. I would have made $72.00 in the time were gone, and Bro. Jarvis and Bro. McAllister would have done as well, or better. Most of the boys, too, were working. The trip was not a success financially, but it paid off in friendship and understanding in the years to come.

I played "Pinky Pinfeathers", a colored roustabout in the play. The troop was complimented everywhere for the fine acting of the characters. This Negro part was right down my alley, as I nearly always played character parts.

We put the play on twice to large audiences after returning to St. George, by which we nearly made up our financial losses.

There were some fine boys in the troop, many of them leaders in this and surrounding counties. To mention a few that I remember and their present activity: Carlyle and Heber Thompson are in the plumbing, sheet metal, appliance and building business in St. George. Roy Condie is an advertising specialist; Bliss Jarvis is with Jennings & Jennings in St. George; George Harmon is a scouter and temple worker. The last time I heard of Ellis McAllister he was teaching L.D.S. religion in an eastern university. It seems this school is absolutely non-sectarian, but encourages all religions and has each religion give a course each year in their religious beliefs. Ellis was selected to teach Mormonism. Carl Condie is local Parcel Post delivery man. Alan Wallis is a High Priest and assistant janitor at the 2nd Ward chapel. Jack Ahlstrom is a prominent dentist at Las Vegas [, Nevada]. Lenzie Sullivan is a postal clerk in the local post office, one of the seven presidents of Seventy and a night ordinance worker at the Temple.

I continued scouting in this troop until March 12th, 1925 when this article appeared in the county paper:

Commissioner B. Glen Smith and Asst. Com. W. C. Cox met with some of the boys of the West Ward at the home of Job F. Hall, Monday night and organized a new troop of Boy Scouts, with Job F. Hall as Scoutmaster and W. C. Cox Assistant Scoutmaster. The designation of the troop is Hiawatha Troop No. 4. Two patrols were organized temporarily with James Andrus and Ivan McGee as patrol leaders and Henry Nichols as scout scribe.

I think it impossible for a man to have fallen in with a better bunch of boys. As I remember, they were James Andrus, Ivan McGee, Henry Nicholes, Eldon Reid, Max McGregor, Clawson

Burgess, Howard Burgess, Culbert Leavy, Grant Miller, and Evan Whitehead. There were perhaps a few others that slip my mind. All of these boys are prominent. James Andrus was bishop of the Second Ward then counselor in the stake presidency, and runs a wagon store in St. George. Ivan McGee is Sec. of Utah Poultry Assoc. at Draper. Henry Nicholes is teaching at an eastern university and so is Culbert Leavy. Eldon Reid is a noted naturalist, Max McGregor is a famous physician of San Francisco and a high councilman in the San Francisco stake, and so it goes all up the line.

I wrote a song, "Hiawatha" and music for it. The melody is in a minor key typical of Native Indian music. I also wrote a patrol song for the Coyote Patrol of which I was patrol leader at a leadership course given at the Dixie College. The Patrols were given 15 minutes to make up a patrol song and be ready to sing it. I had to do this as Carl Moss was the only member of this patrol who knew anything about music. I came up with the following verse set to a melody resembling the coyotes howl:

We are coyotes, outlaws of the range,
That we should admit it may seem very strange.
But if our wild tendencies were rightly directed,
And our natural intelligence trained and perfected,
We may become man's true friend and helpers,
Instead of a pack of aimless wild "yelpers".
Take us, train us, help us, don't maim us.
We may be useful, who knows -- God knows.

I will attach the melody for both of these to this history.
[*Not attached to the original. ed*]

While living in St. George, I took 2 or 3 first-aid courses and got at least two diplomas to teach scouting first-aid. These boys were soon all First Class Scouts and working almost entirely on merit badges. I was scoutmaster until I left St. George in the spring of 1934.

I had a severe sick spell in 1933 and in 1934 went on the road again [selling] for Utah Woolen Mills, but the depression was on and no one, it seemed, had money to buy clothing. I could just barely sell enough to pay my traveling expenses and we were desperately in need of money, so when my brother-in-law, Everest Hackett offered me a job of mining, etc., on his ranch at Deerlodge [near Pioche, Nevada] at $3.00 per day and found, I accepted. I found two boy scouts there, Edward Hackett and Bert Leavy who needed a leader, so I registered with them as supervisor of a lone scout troop. These were good, steady boys and made 2nd and 1st Class and a lot of merit badges that year.

In the fall of 1935, I moved to Panaca, Nevada, where I had work as a carpenter and was immediately inducted into scouting as chairman of the troop committee and Assistant Scoutmaster. I remained in scouting throughout my entire stay at Panaca, mostly as chairman of the troop committee. Two or three years I was a member of the district committee and one year was chairman of the Cathedral Gorge district, B.S.A. I served the last 2 or 3 years as an examiner in merit badge work, and passed most of the boys in their merit badge tests. I was the only man in the district qualified to give the life saving test. I took two courses in Red Cross and one in mine first aid and taught first aid in the scouting and in a citizens training course.

I went on several hikes with the scouts in the absence of the scoutmaster to summer school. On one of these I took a load of the boys in my pickup to Burnt Canyon, about 20 or 30 miles north of Panaca, above Spring Valley. We stayed two nights and had a good time. On the way out we visited places of interest like Rose Valley, Eagle Valley and Spring Valley, all early settlements of the L.D.S. Church and got to Burnt Canyon about mid-afternoon. After pitching our tents we hiked to interesting spots near camp.

I had been here [before] when [I was] a boy 13 or 14 years old with my brother Will, to visit my father, who was herding sheep here for Hide Bros. of Murray, Utah.

The next morning, we climbed the mountain to the north of our camp and as we neared the crest of the hill, the ledge capping the hill looked so red we wondered what the formation was. Imagine our surprise on reaching the ledge to find it covered with red lady bugs. There were hundreds of millions of them on the ledge, completely covering it and in clusters on the trees and scrub oak. There was a large government monument built of rocks on top of the hill and it was completely covered by the red lady bugs. We could have brought them home by the barrel-full if we had been equipped for it.

On another hike, I made with the troop, we went up Condor Canyon between Panaca and Delmues' ranch and examined the old Hebrew writing and drawings on the walls of the canyon, the Phoenician writing and Indian hieroglyphics. On this trip we got permission from Delmues to build a scout cabin at the narrows below their ranch near a big cold spring and to cut cottonwood and black willow trees to make the walls of the cabin. Later, the scoutmaster, Garland Hollingshead, and I went up with some of the boys in my pickup and selected a place to build the cabin and a route for a road to it. But before we could get started, World War II was on and building material [was] rationed so we couldn't do the building. It was not done when I left there in 1951.

One of the greatest thrills of my scouting experience was given me by Rony Jones, who was born just in the lot adjoining mine. (Just through the fence from me.) He saw me every day of his life, caught gophers in my lot, helped me haul hay and dig potatoes, passed nearly every scouting test under me that he made from Tenderfoot to Eagle Scout, passing the last few tests for Eagle rank under me when I was up [there again] after a few things we left when we moved away. Yet he still thinks enough of me to send me a Christmas card last Christmas from Reno, Nevada, where he is going to school.

He won a scholarship last year from the University of Nevada, was married in the St. George temple and his wife and baby are with him in Reno.

On my return to [live in] St. George, in 1951, I was immediately inducted into scouting again, registering as chairman of the troop committee of troop 401, which is the same troop I was made Scoutmaster of on March 12th, 1925. I was registered with this troop from 1951 until October 1956. I didn't re-register this year [1957] because of my failing health. This ended my 35 years in scouting.

However, I did a lot of scout work after returning to St. George. The winter of 1951-52 I taught scouting to the Indian scouts at the Shivwits Indian Reservation, and had charge of their fire building demonstration at the Saparovan held in the Dixie Sun Bowl in May 1952. I worked in the M.I.A. at the reservation that winter with my old friend, Henry Graff. I helped with preparations for the Saparovan every year until 1956, but was laid up with a heart attack then and wasn't physically able to help. That is the reason I didn't register for scout work in October 1956.

Part Five - Church Work

I was baptized in Escalante, Utah, in the Escalante Creek north of town by Ed. Twitchell, who was either bishop or bishop's counselor, and confirmed by Brigham Woolsey. This was 1890.

I was present at a meeting held in Escalante at about this time when the "Manifesto", abolishing polygamy was presented by Pres. Woodruf and accepted by the Escalante Ward. We stayed at the home of Josh Hawkes the night before, as we lived out of town. The grown people had been asked to fast, but Sister Hawkes had prepared breakfast for the children. Before breakfast, my father and brother Hawkes were discussing polygamy. It seemed brother Hawkes was engaged to a girl who was to become his second wife and father was trying to talk him out of going through with it. He intended to marry the girl and move to Mexico. He said [to my Dad], "Will, I love the girl and she loves me, I have my wife's consent to marry her and her consent to become my second wife. And I don't care what the church does about the manifesto, I intended to go through with it as planned."

Just then, Sister Hawkes announced breakfast and we went into the dining room and Bro. Hawkes asked my father to be mouth in prayer. I never heard my father pray as earnestly as he did that morning and when we got up his face had the appearance of an angel. Bro. Hawkes looked at him and said, "Will, I've changed my mind, I wont marry Bertha. I'll vote for the manifesto." This incident made a lasting impression on my mind.

The first church work I remember doing was in the Hebron Ward of the St. George Stake, where I was ordained a deacon when I was 13 years old, by my uncle, Amos P. Hunt. Here I performed the regular duties of a deacon at that time, sweeping out the meeting house, building fires, passing the sacrament and chopping wood for the church building and for widows. I continued these duties at Enterprise, then a branch of the Hebron Ward, and acted as chorister of the Sunday School and Primary. In the fall of 1903 I went to Hatch, Utah where Annie Clove lived to whom I was engaged to be married. I had brought a recommend with me to the Hatch Ward, and performed the duties of a deacon here until in October when I was ordained an Elder by Wm. R. Riggs, as we intended to get married in the temple.

We were married in the St. George Temple on Oct. 27, 1903. We went through again the next day for some of Annie's ancestors. We visited in Enterprise a few days then returned to Hatch to make our home. Here I labored as a Ward Teacher, taught a class in Sunday School, in Mutual [M.I.A] and in the Aaronic division of priesthood meeting, and served as Sunday School chorister. I was Supervisor of Religion Classes in the Hatch Ward one or two years, and Annie and I both taught in this organization.

I had an experience in Hatch that was unusual. I served a while as assistant to the bishop. Bishop Ross Lynn could neither read nor write, his first counselor, but very little, and the wife of his second counselor was in a critical condition with cancer of the stomach which tied him home and the ward clerk lived on a ranch out of town. It was necessary that some one in town read the bishop's letters from church headquarters, advise with him on them and answer them, so the stake president appointed me, Bishop's Assistant. Bishop Lynn was the best bishop I ever knew and kept well posted on the news of the world and the progress of the church by having someone read to him. His wife and his daughter-in-law, Polly Lynn, read to him from the newspaper, Improvement Era, Juvenile Instructor, but it was parts of my duties to keep him up to date on the progress of the church. I also served here as president of the Y.M.M.I.A and as assistant superintendent of the Sunday School. I was sustained as a member of the stake Sunday school board, but only attended one meeting of the board when the stake was reorganized and a new Sunday school board was selected.

In the fall of 1906, I was called on a mission to the Southern States. But I worked so hard and wallowed [in] so much snow getting a new store building near enough finished so I could move the store goods into it before I left that I just about broke my health down, and left with a bad cold and some bad festered sores on my hands. Leaving Hatch where there was three or four feet of snow and sub-zero weather and going down into Mississippi where it was hotter in the winter sometimes than it ever got in Hatch in the summer seemed to be too much of a shock to my system, because the festered sores healed right up and my cough stopped, but I developed cystitis, which soon got so bad I couldn't walk to go tracting. So I was sent in to the mission headquarters at Meridian, so I could be under the care of a good doctor. But the doctor gave no hope of me recovering in less than a year, so I was released and sent home in March, 1907. I left home about the 10th of December, 1906.

I was active as a ward teacher and teacher in Sunday school during the summer of 1907, but my health wasn't too good and Dr. Clark of Panguitch advised me to go to a warmer climate, so we sold the store and moved back to Enterprise. I was immediately inducted into service as a ward teacher and a teacher in M.I.A. and priesthood work. For two or three years I was presiding teacher over the Clovervalley Branch of the Enterprise Ward and was responsible for three visits per year, at the least, being made to this branch. I usually had to go myself, sometimes alone, as it was a long distance and the trip had to be made by team and buggy or on horseback, and a person was gone from Saturday morning until Monday night.

In the spring of 1921, I traded my ranch at Hebron and cattle, [a] team and all farm equipment for part of the Bastian farm at Washington. Here, I served as ward and Sunday school chorister, and ward, Sunday school, and M.I.A. teacher and drama coach for the Mutuals, as I had had a lot of experience in that work. We also did a lot of temple work, and finished the endowments and sealings for all the names we had. The baptism work had been done before by my father's uncle, Charles Hall, and his wife, Susan, and others.. I also filled a stake mission while here in the wards of Toquerville and Laverkin. We found a lot of [people with the] flu in Toquerville and endeared ourselves to the people by our work with the sick. Bro. Wm. Bunting was my companion. It was at Washington that I began my scouting activities which lasted 35 years.

We moved from here to St. George in the fall of 1923 where I continued the same church work that I did in Washington, and in addition, served on the ward genealogical board as assistant superintendent, and also as a missionary, being on the Stake Home Missionary list. I was also ordained a Seventy while living here. Financial conditions got so bad here during the depression that I was forced to leave in the spring of 1934 and go into Nevada where I could find employment. We settled in Panaca in 1935 and I was used in about the same church capacities that I had been active in in St. George. In addition, I was ordained a High Priest and served six years as Ward Clerk under two bishops, was in the Sunday School superintendency as Assistant Superintendent of Sunday School four times, was a Home Missionary ward chairman and Stake Chairman of Genealogy, ward, then stake building supervisor, member stake auditing committee, secretary of the stake ward teachers and Adult Aaronic Priesthood committee, stake store keeper and a member of the Stake High Council.

In the spring of 1951, we bought a home in St. George and moved back there on Thanksgiving day, that fall. We had started to do temple work for the dead again and found it a long drive from Panaca to St. George and return, about 210 miles. On returning here [to St. George] we began going to the temple Wednesday and Thursday nights. My first church appointment was working in the M.I.A. at the Shivwits Indian reservation which I did for about a year or two. Then I joined the New England Historic Genealogical Society of Boston and began doing genealogical research work. I was a member of the ward genealogical committee as assistant superintendent until Bishop Nelson was released when a new committee was organized.

Through my research work I have had over two thousand names processed for temple work and the baptisms and endowments done Fortnum, and most of the sealing work has been done. I am currently serving as secretary of the High Priests Quorum of the Second Ward, St. George Stake.

Part Six - Public Offices I have held

Political and Civil

I was elected Constable in the Hatch [Utah] Precinct about 1904 and served in this capacity until I left there in the fall of 1907. I only made one arrest that I remember of and carry the scar of the stab in my arm by a small knife in the hands of a Mexican laborer. He got quite a stiff fine over it. All the other work I did as constable was rounding up wild horses and selling them at auction under the law, then after the expense of advertising and feed was paid, the money was split between the constable and the county, the county's share going into the school fund.

I sold quite a few horses and became quite proficient as a horse auctioneer. I also served as postmaster of Hatch during the same period. I was selected about this time as a member of a committee of three to protest the method of construction of the Hatch Reservoir being built by the D. B. Brinton Co. for the State of Utah under contract. The contract specified, as did the specifications, that a trench be dug across the canyon from hill to hill, to bedrock and a clay puddle core put in the center of the dam to cut off seepage.

When the company started to work they found quicksand all over the old canyon bottom at about two or three feet above water level. So Mr. Brinton talked the State's Engineer into letting him drive timbers two inches thick, edge to edge to bedrock across the channel as it was very difficult and expensive to dig a trench to bedrock under the conditions. Sam Barnhurst and I had visited the work soon after they had started to drive these timbers, which were 2x4, 2x6 and 2x8 pine bought at a local saw mill.

These timbers were sharpened and started edge to edge but didn't drive that way to any depth. One would strike a cobble rock in the sand and turn upstream and its companion would strike one and turn downstream, so that by the time they reached bedrock, about ten feet down or more, the bottom ends would be [from] one to four feet apart. We protested this but were disregarded, so a mass meeting of the people of Hatch and Hillsdale was called at which Sam Barnhurst, Wm. Wilson and I were appointed as a committee representing the two towns (Wilson was from Hillsdale) to wait on the contractor and engineer and make a formal protest of the method and have the protest acknowledged.

This was Saturday night. Monday morning, I wrote up a formal protest in which I specified that if the protest was not heeded, the state would be held responsible for all damage done in case the reservoir should break because of this slipshod method of construction. Mr. Wilson was taken suddenly ill Sunday so was unable to go with us, but Sam Barnhurst and I went up Monday and presented the protest. The state's engineer said there was no danger so signed the protest for us, acknowledging receipt of it.

But just a few years later, the reservoir [dam] did go out suddenly because of this very thing. Water began seeping through these timbers as soon as the head gate was closed at the dam to fill the pond and kept increasing in volume until nearly as much was running out as was running in. The morning [the dam] went out, about three years after completion, Dimick Huntington, the watchman reported over telephone from the dam that this seepage had suddenly become roily, and warned people below to evacuate low homes and get all livestock out of low corrals or pastures, as the dam might go any minute.

People evacuated low homes and got their horses, milk cows, calves and pigs out of low corrals, but before cattle could be moved from pastures the dam, as Mr. Huntington told [the dam], "just raised up and let the water go under and the dam fell back into the pond. The water was only one hour reaching Panguitch, 20 miles away, and as my Uncle, Al. Riding told it to me [the water] came as a wall about 20 feet high, rolling trees and willows in front of it. He said it was traveling so fast that large cottonwood trees broke off like pipe stems before the water touched them just from the force of air in front of this wall.

Some Panguitch citizens [had] fastened the new wood bridge across the river east of Panguitch [attaching it] to some large cottonwood trees with chains in an effort so save the bridge. That summer the bridge was found in a field near Circleville. The chains were still on but the bridge was badly damaged. The presenting of the protest proved a wise move as the state had to pay all damage and loss caused by the dam breaking.

Quite a few cattle and horses were drowned, but no human lives were lost. No homes were washed away as the force of the water against the hill above Hatch caused the water to swing to the east and miss the town, although the water line on the hill east of Hatch was higher than some of the homes in town. The water swung to the west again just above Hillsdale and that little town was spared also. I had [had] the protest recorded in the County Recorders office at Panguitch.

The next public office I remember holding was clerk of the town of Enterprise. I signed all the bonds in a bond issue sold to the Palmer Bond and Mortgage Co. of New York, but one wouldn't recognize the signature. I signed my name then like this: Job F. Hall. I changed to my present signature later, thus, Job F. Hall. [In the manuscript of this history, the first is more elegantly formed, while the second is more like ordinary hand writing fr.]

At this time I was appointed Special Deputy Sheriff of Washington County, as a safety measure adopted by the county during World War I. John I. Pace and Alma Nelson were appointed Special Deputies at the same time. I made three arrests as Deputy Sheriff, one a real German spy I overtook on his way to blow up the head house of the Enterprise water system. Some children reported seeing the man headed that way, so I got on my old brown work horse and followed him.

When I caught up with him he was nearing a point [bend] in the road so I just galloped on by waving friendly at him as I went, but stopped and turned the horse off the road and facing back toward him when I got around the first point . When he came around the point, I had him covered with my .38 Colts which I wore in a belt over my right shoulder with the gun under my left arm under my coat. I made him walk back to town in front of me and turned him over to Arthur Huntsman, Constable of Enterprise.

In examining the contents of a small grip he was carrying, we found maps of the Enterprise culinary water system, the Enterprise reservoir, irrigation head dams of Bunkerville and Mesquite [, Nevada] on the Virgin River and the head houses of the Las Vegas water system, with orders to blow them up and plenty of explosives to do it with. He was sent to Fort Douglas for the duration of the war.

The next arrest I made was an old man and two grown sons who came to Enterprise about six weeks later, selling bible encyclopedias. The old man was tall and very straight for a grey-haired man, and looked like a Prussian Nobleman. The sons were large healthy looking men, about 20 and 22 year old. The three deputies were notified of their arrival, so we got together to decide what to do about them. We had no German interpreter in Enterprise so decided that I should watch their cabin for the night then we would get Willard Jones from New Castle to come over the next day and examine their papers when we arrested them.

These men had rented a cabin in the NW quarter of Enterprise in which they were staying. I watched the cabin that night in near zero temperature, (it was about the first of December). The next day the other deputies felt like there was no danger from them, so refused to make an arrest. But when night came they were filled with fears again and asked me to ride herd on the cabin again. The reason they gave for not doing right duty was that one of them had just recovered from pneumonia and the other had a house full of sick children.

These conditions of fear and ease continued until I had watched the place three nights, part of the time laying against the building to see if I could hear them say anything that would incriminate them. So after the third watch, I arrested them and marched them over in town. Just as we got into Main Street I saw Willard Jones drive to the post office so took the men there. We met Willard just as he came out of the post office and I told him what I wanted and deputized him to look through their papers.

He examined their papers and talked with the old man in German, then he told me that there was nothing in the papers to indicate that they were spies. In fact, most of the papers were written in English. The old man told Willard That they belonged to the L.D.S. Church, that he was a convert from Germany, that both boys had filled missions for the church that they both had weak hearts and failed to pass the test for army life.

He [further] said they lived neighbors to Anthony W. Ivins in Salt Lake [City] and would pay for a telephone to President Ivins. I accepted the offer and sent a ten word message to Apostle Ivins. I got an answer back almost immediately saying he would vouch for the man and that a letter would follow. The next morning I was given a night message from President or Apostle Ivins confirming all the old gentleman had told Willard and I. So, of course, I apologized and turned them loose. They came to priesthood meeting that week and the following Sunday spoke in meeting. They were all very well posted on the gospel.

The third arrest I made was at or near my ranch north of Enterprise the next spring. I was up in my field plowing when I saw a team coming up through the field on an old road, with two men in the wagon. I went over to the road and stopped them and asked where they were going. They avoided the question and gave various vague answers but left me with the impression that they didn't want me to know where they were going.

So I watched them and after they got out of my field they headed south through the brush and went directly toward a high peak south of my ranch. We had been warned to be on the lookout for German spies who had been sent out to poison cattle feed yards in Southern Utah and Eastern Nevada. I had noted that these men were well armed and well provisioned, and that from this peak, using field glasses, they could spot all the feed yards to the east, and then slip out by night on horseback and poison them. So of course, I reasoned they were the spies we had been warned about.

Therefore, I unhitched my team from the plow and went down to my stable and unharnessed them and put one in its stall. I then put the saddle and bridle on my bay saddle mare and went to the house and told my wife I was going to follow these men, that I had put the saddle on Pet and if I wasn't back in two hours, or if she heard any shooting up at the foot of the peak she was to send [my daughter] Grace on the mare for help.

I rode Old Chief, the same horse I was riding when I made the first arrest at Enterprise. I went directly to their camp and made a cursory examination of the contents of the wagon. I noticed a box of stock pellets, a box of dynamite, and some caps and fuse, and two saddles. I listened a little and could hear the men up on the peak so I rode up the ravine in the east side of the peak. My horse seemed so sense the need of caution, so walked very quietly. After going quite a distance up this ravine, I caught sight of the men through the timber and noted that they were headed toward the ravine, and would strike it at about a [certain] large pine tree in the bottom of the ravine, so I rode on up to the tree and waited.

As they came out into the ravine I pointed the .38 at them and commanded them to reach for the sky and arrested them in the name of the State of Utah. It was a man about 45 years old and his son, about 20. The man asked what they had done, and I told him I thought they were German spies. He heaved a sigh and said if that was all I wanted they were all right. I slipped off my horse, keeping them covered and he handed me a letter saying it would clear everything up.

The letter was from Harry Thorley of Cedar City [, Utah] hiring him to go plow some land on Thorley's sheep ranch east of Modena and sow some rye he would find in the granary on the ranch. I knew Harry Thorley and his signature, having seen it many times on checks when I worked for B. J. Lund Co. in Modena. After reading the letter I released the men, but asked them why they didn't tell me that when I stopped them down in my field.

Mr. Harris, (it was Nage Harris) said his son had found some good looking float [(?)] on the peak when he was herding sheep there for Thorley the fall before, and they wanted to find the vein and shoot into it a little before going on over to plow. That accounted for the dynamite. The box of stock pellets was repacked with eggs. When I got back to the house my two hours was nearly up and Grace was getting ready to go for help. It was a happy family I had returned to.

About this time my brother-in-law, Ivor Clove, and I joined the C. J. Ludwig Detective Agency of Kansas City, Missouri. I think Ivor quit at the end of the first year, but I stayed with them for 24 years, acting as a secret agent for them in Enterprise and in St. George. I made no arrests for them but gave secret information that lead to the arrest of many people. While serving as deputy Sheriff of Washington County, I was appointed deputy Sheriff of Iron County, as well and in this capacity broke up a notorious cattle stealing ring that was operating on the Escalante Desert, north of Enterprise.

Two men of Enterprise, two from Newcastle, three from Cedar City, some from Lund and vicinity and one or two from Milford were implicated. The boys from Enterprise would go out and ride through a bunch of cattle north of Enterprise and give them a little start north. An hour or so later the Newcastle pair would strike the same bunch and do the same thing, and succeeding men would do the same until the cattle were somewhere south of Lund when they would be taken and driven to Frisco in cattle cars on the railroad and shipped east or to California and sold as feeders.

The Beaver County brand inspector and a certain railroad freight crew were involved when the trap was sprung. I also gave information that resulted in the arrest and conviction of a local Iron County man for stealing cattle and sheep.

I was sustained as Justice of the Peace of the Lund Precinct while working for H. J. Doolittle Co., and served as interpreter for the sheriff, doctor and prosecuting attorney when some Mexicans were killed there in an automobile accident. One white man was also killed and the driver of the car, a Vehlie [(?)] seven passenger touring car, in the accident. I also acted as a postal clerk in the post office at Lund and as assistant manager of the H. J. Doolittle Co.

I guess the next public office I held was president of the Panaca Irrigation Company, for a six-year period. I was elected as a "spite" move because I had criticized the lax methods of the existing Board of Directors. I adopted a new policy and made such a wonderful success of it that I was retained [for the] six years. While president we replaced nearly all head gates, raised the wages from $5.00 to $8.00 per day, doubled the water master's salary, stopped all the leaks in the concrete pipe line. We were also instrumental in getting a culinary water system for Panaca which enabled us to cut off all the individual water systems from the concrete pipe line, thus saving about 25 or 30 miners inches of water for the irrigation company, and had, as I remember it, $685.00 in the bank.

There was not enough money in the bank to cover the outstanding checks when we tool over. We went onto a cash basis immediately when we were elected, and collected all assessments and did this without raising the assessment. I have held no public offices since.

In 1932 or 1933 I made an audit of the books of the county clerk at the request of the state. My audit showed that the clerk had the right amount of money but didn't know how to keep books[!]. I also made a business audit of all stores and farm machinery dealers in Washington County for the US Government. I also served as Assistant County Bee Inspector for 1922 to 1924.

See, I have forgotten to mention that I played baseball a lot and served several years as captain of the Enterprise baseball team. I also did quite a lot of umpiring. I was a good pitcher, and threw a ball that was never knocked out of the diamond. Also threw an in[side] curve that was awfully hard to hit. I injured my arm at Lund, Utah in 1918 in a matched baseball game, and I never recovered from the injury, so never pitched afterwards. We won the game that day, 5 to 4 and all the real support I had was a old league catcher, George Southerland. I struck the other side out in all but one inning.

I was also manager of the Washington town baseball team for two years.

Part Seven – Miscellaneous

[Note: Judging from certain events described, this part of the history was probably written later, about 1956. gfr]

In reading over the history of my life, I find that I have left out some interesting items, so I am recording them here. They are probably not in chronological order, for I am recording each one as they come to me.

In writing of my childhood I have failed to say that one of our playmates was Chinaman, the son of Chief Bishop of the Indian tribe of Escalante. He wanted to teach us the Indian language but our stand was that we teach him English, as there was only one of him and about ten of us.

Neither have I told of the petrified trees lying on winter quarters hill between our farm and Escalante. These trees had axe marks in them that had been made before they petrified. Neither have I told of the caves in the sandstone cliffs at the forks of North Creek and the upper potatoe valley creek, and how we found the entrance to these caves when we were hunting arrow heads on top of the cliff. This entrance was a crack in the sandstone down which one could go to the caves below by tensing the back and knees against the sides of the crack. One could climb up the same way. It was really one enormous cave divided into 10 or 12 rooms by partitions of small stones that were plastered with clay and glazed as smooth as crockery with some substance almost as transparent as glass.

Nor have I told of the men on foot and on horses, and of dogs drawn on the smooth face of the cliff with something that resembled colored chalk. Most of these were red, but some were blue or yellow. Nor of how we tried to wash these off but couldn't, yet they looked as if they had been drawn the day before with colored chalk. Nor have I told of the cave farther down the canyon and on the apposite side, with a stake and rider fence across the face of it; nor how my brother Will and Jode Porter cut steps in the cliff with their pocket knives and climbed up to it, a distance of about 20 feet, wearing [out] the blades of their knives doing so. They were rewarded with only a few arrowheads and some pottery and corn cobs.

Nor have I told of the time my brother Will and I went about a mile from our ranch one night after dark and climbed a tall Pinion Pine tree and watched an Indian burial, and how one of their dogs nearly "gave us away" by looking that way and barking. But an old squaw saved us by saying the dog could smell a coyote. The Indian, whose burial we watched was one Frank Spaniard, a gambler, who won a lot of money in Arizona, New and Old Mexico by gambling.

He had a beautiful pinto horse with white mane and tail and spent most of his winnings for silver ornaments for his saddle, bridle and pistol holster. We saw them put this dead Indian in the grave, put his blankets, gun, a nearly new .44 Winchester rifle, and his gambling paraphernalia in with him, then lead the beautiful pinto horse with the saddle and bridle on, and his pistol in its holster hung on the horn of the saddle, out by the grave and shoot him and roll him in with his master, then cover them up with dirt and pile rocks on top to prevent coyotes, etc., from digging into it. During all this time the squaws and some of the bucks were keeping up a continual howling, as the Israelites did of old.

Neither have I told how my brother, Will, wanted to go dig into this grave a few days later, after the Indians had moved away and recover the saddle and bridle and gun. Nor how my father would have none of it, telling us that had the Indians discovered us that night they would have shot us and buried us, too, and that if the least hint ever got out that we had watched the ceremony, our lives and perhaps the lives of the entire family wouldn't be worth a pinch of snuff! This is the first time I ever heard about it.

Nor have I told of how the next day after the burial, Will and I saw some squaws on a hill below our farm chasing something along a low ledge, and throwing rocks at what ever they were chasing, and of how occasionally we would hear a howl or scream coming from that direction. After the squaws left we got on a horse and rode down to investigate and there under the ledge was a young squaw that had been killed with rocks, with a heap of large rocks piled on her body.

From what one of the squaws told mother and Chinaman, the chief's son told Will and I there was a connection between the death of Frank Spaniard and the young squaw. One of the squaws told mother that under their tribal law if a young squaw got into trouble and was going to have a papoose before she was married, she was run out of the camp and given one day to go hunt another tribe, but after a day and night the squaws of her tribe were to hunt for her, and if they found her they were to kill here with rocks. If she got to another tribe she was free.

But though another tribe was obliged to take her in and care for her and the papoose when it arrived, they must live in a wigwam by themselves, and no one would marry either of them. Chinaman told Will and I that Frank Spaniard had broken the tribal law, and after he did he got awful sick and died. He was probably shot in tribal law.

Nor have I told of the week I spent with my uncle, Robert F. Hall at the saw mill, where he was hauling logs with oxen. Nor how I worried when the whistle blew the first evening at six o'clock, and he stopped and unyoked the oxen and turned them loose in the timber, after putting a bell on one of each yoke. He had 3 yoke, six oxen. I wondered how he would ever get them back to the wagon the next morning and get them yoked up again. It was no trouble to find them with bells on and I noticed that each yoke were by themselves.

When we got to the first yoke my uncle just told them to "get up" and gave the command, "Gee" or "Haw" and drove them to the second pair, and then these four were driven to the third pair and all to the wagon. When he hitched them up he just called one name and said, "Get in there". This ox went in beside the wagon tongue. Then he told his mate to get in, and he went in on the other side of the tongue. He then put the yoke on these and commanded the next pair to get in, and put the yoke on them and the same with the last pair, hitching them up about as quick as I have written about it.

When he loaded a log, he drove parallel to it and about twelve feet away, then placed two poles called skids with one end on the wagon wheel and the other end near the log. He had a chain about 30 feet long with hooks on each end and a ring in the center. The hooks were fastened to rings in the bulkhead on the wagon and the ring in the center of the chain was passed under the log and another chain hooked into this ring. Then the chain the lead yoke of oxen pulled on was unhooked from the main draft chain and this yoke of oxen was driven around on the opposite side of the wagon and their draft chain hooked to this loading chain, thus the oxen being driven forward away from the wagon rolled the log up the skids onto the wagon.

The end timbers of the bulkhead which rested on top of the front and rear bolsters of the wagon were hollowed out some on top so the log would not roll off.

It doesn't seem possible that an animal as dumb as a cow apparently is, can be taught to obey orders as an ox does. My uncle could drive this ox team of 3 yoke so the wagon would be within six inches of where he wanted it just by giving the commands used in driving oxen.

Just after Christmas in 1900 or 1901 my father and I started to Delamar with Tommy Terry to hunt work. When we got as far as Clovervalley, George Edwards had just taken a contract to get out a quantity of mine timbers for the Delamar Mine, and needed choppers. As my father and I were expert axemen we took a contract to go chop mine timbers for him for three cents per lineal foot. So he took us out to an old saw mill setting about 16 miles south of Clovervalley where there was quite a lot of good timber. At this old setting was a fairly good dugout [house], though small, (about 8x10 feet) which we fixed up to sleep in and store our provisions, but cooked on an open fire outside.

There had been about 18 inches of snow fall before Christmas, then it had warmed up and rained a little and turned real cold again and froze the snow so solid it would support a team and wagon, so we had not trouble getting to this old mill site. We got along without incident until Valentine's Day, February 14th. When we got up this morning it was snowing hard but we continued to chop timber as long as we could wallow the snow, thinking every day it would quit. But when the snow got too deep to get out of camp we were worried because our supplies were getting low, and prospects of getting out for supplies or Bro. Edwards getting in with more looked very poor.

So we started discussing the possibilities of making skis to get out. Neither of us had ever been on skis, but we reasoned that the first man who used them had to learn and we believed we were as smart and camp-wise as he was. So we dug into the old edging pile at the mill and got some straight-grained edgings and made some skis. We made a trial trip close on these, but father broke one of his so we cut [down] a straight quakenasp [quaking aspen tree] that grew by our camp and he made a pair out of it. These stood a test run, so we were ready to go. In fact we had to go as we had only food enough left after breakfast the next morning for one meal, and the snow was now six feet deep and it was still snowing.

We put all our cooking utensils in the dugout, fixed a lunch of our last food and started for Clovervalley about ten o'clock, a.m. It was still snowing and the snow was so soft we would sink nearly to our knees in it, then the snow would fall in on the skis behind you and freeze to them, so the leader was dragging about 10 to 20 pounds of snow part of the time. We, of course, took turns breaking trail.

When we got to the active saw mill about two miles from our camp, we found that two other men had been camped there, too, chopping timber but left for Clovervalley when it first started to snow, expecting us to do the same. There was a bed here in the camp house and a little food, consisting of a piece of ham, flour and baking powder, but there were two or three dead mice on the floor and we were afraid that food they left had been poisoned to kill the mice, so we were afraid to stop here and use it.

We did each take a piece of bacon rind from the table to grease our skis to prevent snow from sticking to them. This helped a little, but didn't last long. About four o'clock, p.m., it quit snowing and at sundown we could see it was clearing up. Then a north breeze came and it turned extremely cold. We stopped twice and tried to build a fire, intending to stay by a fire all night, but everything was too wet so we were forced to keep going or freeze to death.

When we got within about two miles of Barclay I got warm and sleepy, or felt warm and told pa I would just lay down there and sleep until morning then come on in, but he knew these were the signals of freezing to death, so [he] punched me with his ski pole and made me get up and go on. I wondered what made him get so mean to me all at once. About a mile farther on we run into open trail where cattle had been driven out from town to graze on the buck brush and cliff rose shrubbery that grew abundantly in the old tufa formation here. We stuck our skis in a tree and went on in this trail. The jar of our feet in the packed trail helped to revive us, and we soon began to get really warmer. It was four o'clock a.m. when we got to Jap [?] Wood's home in Clovervalley or Barclay as the town is now called. Having just eaten snow to quench or thirst all day we were very thirsty. We broke the ice on a bucket of water to get a drink and I was still so cold the water with ice floating in it seemed warm to me.

We stayed here a few days and while here cleaned the snow off of the roof of the house and shoveled some trail and chopped up a pile of wood., as Brother Woods was away at Delamar working.

Then we borrowed two rangy horses and carrying our skis in front of us set out one morning for Enterprise, about 35 miles to the east. The going was slow, as the snow was deep, but by keeping on the south brink of the ridges where the wind had blown the snow off a little we found it easier for the horses than to try to follow the road.

It was nearly sundown when we got to the top of the summit, where we turned our mounts loose and prepared to go on by man power. We ate a lunch we had brought with us, then put on our skis and started on. We made good progress for a short time as the snow would support us on our skis, but it soon became dark and we run into trouble. All the brush were covered with snow and the terrain looked even and smooth in the darkness of the cloudy moonless night, but first one then the other of us would fall into a wash, so we became alarmed for fear of breaking a leg or an arm and stopped under a big half dead cedar tree which we cut down with a small axe we were carrying, made a fire with the dead wood and scattered the green limbs around to stand on. When I stepped off my skis under this tree the snow was right up to my arm pits.

We stayed by this fire until the moon came up, then started on. We could see a peak to the east of us and knew that the wagon road crossed the pass at the south base of this peak, so we headed for the peak and came into the road just a t daylight. We could follow the line of this road through the trees and reached Terry's Ranch just as Tommy Terry had breakfast ready. And we were ready to eat it! He was here alone feeding cattle and was glad of some company and an opportunity to send a letter out to his family. After breakfast and a short rest we went on and reached home about one-thirty p.m., worn out, dead for sleep and glad to be home again.

After resting a few days, Johnny Alger and I got on the skis and went to the Calf Spring Ranch, about six miles south of Enterprise, which Algers owned, to see how the horses and cattle they had left there were faring. We got up there about one o'clock and ate a lunch. Their two saddle mares were in the corral eating old hay and straw off the shed. We fed them before going to the house. Then after lunch we got on these horses and went down about a quarter of a mile to where Pilot Peak canyon came in and tried to go up the canyon but found a drift of snow too deep to get through.

We then went back to the ranch and left the horses, as we found them to be quite weak, and put on the skis and went up in the upper end of the field, in hopes we would find the cattle there, but they weren't. The next morning a big light-red cow was in the corral, having come from toward the mouth of Pilot Peak canyon. So after Breakfast we put on the skis and went down there again, and up the canyon about 100 yards we found the rest of the cattle all dead in the wash, under a mammoth bunch of service berry brush that grew on the bank of the wash. These brush were 15 or 20 feet tall and the snow had bent them down over the wash making perfect shelter like a shed or stable, but with no feed in it.

Evidently, the cattle had gone into this sheltered spot for protection from the snow and cold and had all starved and frozen to death. They had eaten the sage brush all up, and had eaten oak and service berry limbs from 3/4 to one inch in diameter. The old red cow's tracks looked as though she had gone to each of the dead ones and smelled of them and tried to get them to get up and go with her. As I recall it there were 15 head of young cattle here from six months to 18 months old. A lot of cattle and horses suffered the same fate on the range that winter.

Another experience worth recording was one associated Johnny Alger. We had bought a shingle mill and cut a few shingles late one fall at Hatch, and left with a load of shingles for Enterprise. Before we got to Panguitch it began to cloud up and looked like snow was due, so we sold the shingles to my uncle Al Riding in Panquitch for fear we would get caught in a bad snow storm in Bearvalley, which we did. Uncle Al wanted us to stay over in Panquitch a few days until the weather looked better, saying he could use us on a house he was building if we wanted to stay. He was a building contractor. But we were anxious to get through and thought we could make it with four horses and an empty wagon and [so we] pushed on.

It began snowing on us before we got to Bearvalley and was snowing quite hard when we reached the upper ranch the first night out from Panguitch. It snowed about two feet that night, and the wind was blowing the next morning, drifting the snow. We left early and when we got out about a mile we found the washes drifted full of snow and so many marks of roads in the brush that we couldn't tell which was the road, so I got out and walked ahead of the team to be sure we didn't drop into a wash that was an old road.

When we got to the top of the summit I was wet to the waist , but soon dried out when we stopped for noon down in a warm cave in Little Creek canyon. We stayed with Dick Lund in Paragoonah that night, and camped the nest night out on the cedar bottoms. The second night out we camped on Sand Spring ridge. It was extremely cold here, as the snow was about six inches deep and crusted and a cold north wind blowing, with nothing to make fire with but shadscale and greasewood.

We did manage to eat a little supper by a small fire then John and Mary, his wife, who was my sister, and their baby Cecil went to bed in the wagon, but I tried to sleep on a canvas cot set up on the snow. I couldn't keep warm this way, so got up and folded the cot right down on the snow, I did get a little sleep this way but got so cold about four a.m. that I got up and hitched up my team and started on, leading Johnny's team behind the wagon. We got along without incident until we got up by the Newcastle fields at the mouth of Pinto canyon.

On of my lines was real short, and I dropped it some way here and the team started to follow a cattle trail along the fence, and I couldn't pull them away from the fence as the line I still had was on the fence side. I showed John the one line and he understood the condition at once and grabbed this line and I jumped out over the near horse and caught him by the bits and stopped the team, and just in time, for had we gone ten feet farther, wagon and all would have tumbled into a wash about twelve feet deep.

Just after we got back into the road we saw a pile of drift wood the summer floods had left, so we stopped and made a good fire and ate dinner. We changed teams after dinner, but as soon as we got to Enterprise I got a strap about two feet long and riveted it to that short line of mine. Bearvalley was always a "bugaboo" to travelers, mud in the spring and summer and snow in the winter.

I haven't told of the time [my wife] Annie and I got stuck in the mud on the Bearvalley hill and how a sheepman came along riding a big work horse and hitched the horse in with my best one and helped us nearly up the hill when my horse got discouraged because the sheepman made such long pulls, and how Annie rode behind him on his horse to Paragoonah because one of my horses wasn't broke to ride, and how Ben Watts went back with me the next day and got my wagon.

Nor of the time I rounded a point in the long valley and almost ran into a load of lumber stuck in the mud and how my wagon went down in the mud when I turned out to pass this loaded wagon and how I unhitched from my stuck wagon and hitched my team on lead of the other man's team and helped him out, only to have him drive off and leave me there with my wagon stuck in the mud. I've never seen this man since as I was headed west and he, east. It took me about two hours to get my wagon out of this mud hole.

In my general history I mention spending the winter of 1914-15 in Escalante, having intended to buy an interest in my brothers store and stay there. I just say I found the store wouldn't pay two families so I left. Well, I left [out of my history] some experiences on this trip that I think should be told. I left [town] in the company of three other men, two of these men had wives with them and were going to Antimony. The other man, Parley Riddle, was just going to help them over the mountain as we had to load our wagons on bob sleds at Mitchell's Shingle Mill to get over the mountain.

We reached this mill early the second day out and loaded Black's wagon on one set of bobs and Riddle went right on with it as he had to get to Antimony that night. The other two men stayed and helped me get my wagon on another set of bobs, and insisted on me hitching my big team on wheel and the small team on lead against my judgment, then one of them was going to show me how to drive four horses, and turned my leaders back beside the wheel team and got one of my wheel horses excited so he refused to go, then rode off and left me.

I let them stand a while after straightening them up, then got on and drove into the creek we had to cross right there but bob sleds are hard to pull on a rocky creek bed. Something like pulling a cross-locked wagon. The left front runner on Brownie's side hit a rock which throbbed the tongue against him and he stopped. I had either rubber boots or high-top overshoes on so didn't get my feet wet when I got out in the creek and unhitched the teams and drove them out, then carried Annie and the children, Grace and Priscilla, across the creek. I hitched Net, my little bay mare, and Dick, the big black gelding to the bobs, tying Dick's doubletree back to the roller on the bobs with a chain and pulled the bobs out of the creek.

Then I hitched the team up like I wanted to in the first place with Buck, a yellow gelding and Net on "wheel" and the big team, Dick and Brownie, (the team I mention elsewhere in this history of pulling a six-foot McCormick grain binder with), on lead and had no more trouble, until I got several miles farther on to a steep pitch that faced the south and was bare of snow, up which my teams couldn't pull the bobs. I knew Parley Riddle would soon be back, so took Dick and Brownie and went back to the shingle mill and got my white top buggy. When I got back to the bobs, Parley had got there and was trying to pull the bobs up the pitch by zigzagging on it.

I hitched my team on lead of his and the four big horses had no trouble pulling the bobs up the hill. We then hitched my little tam on the buggy for Annie to drive and went on to the foot of the mountain where we camped for the night. The next morning we hitched Riddle's team and my big team on my bobs and took my wagon over the mountain and left Annie and the children with it while we went back for my buggy, taking the bobs back with us. After looking things over, Parley and I decided we could save him a trip back over the mountain by chopping two small quaking aspen poles and anchoring my buggy to them in place of the bobs. So we did this, and put the wheels inside the buggy, hitched my four horses to the buggy and Parley went with me a ways up the mountain to see how things worked. I found I could go right along this way so Parley and I settled up for the use of the bobs and his help and he went back, intending to stay at the shingle mill that night where he would leave the bobs.

We had loaded his wagon on the bobs when we decided to use quakenasps under my buggy. It was almost dark when I got back over to my wagon and Annie had almost collapsed with fear. She imagined she could hear a bear moving around in a grove of thick pines about fifty yards from the wagon. She actually had streaks of grey come in her hair over it. We went on from there the next day and on the second day at noon arrived at the small town of Kingston. This was the day we expected to be at Enterprise when we left Escalante, and had arrived here, where I knew no one, without feed for the horses, nor food for ourselves, and I was broke, as it took all the money I had to pay Mr. Riddle.

I went over to the store and found that it was owned and operated by Bishop Allen of the Kingston L.D.S. Ward. I told him frankly of the condition I was in, and asked him if he would take my check for some supplies and hold it until I could get home an sell some hay and get the money in the bank. He asked me who I knew that he knew. I named a few boys who had gone to school at Beaver when I did, from Kingston, and he said, "You know some good boys,

I'll take a chance on you". So I got a few bales of hay and a sack of oats, and a few groceries. My purchases amounted to between $7.00 and $8.00, so he said to write the check for $10.00, as I might need a dollar or so before I got home.

The next day after I got home, I went up in town and one of the first men I met wanted to buy a small stack of hay I had, so I sold it, sent the money to the Bank and wrote and told Bishop Allen that his check was good. I saw his son, DeValson, here a year or so ago. He was one of the men I told Bishop Allen I knew. I got a nice letter back from Bishop Allen. I have never seen him since, but feel sure I shall see him and associate with him in that life that is to come.

But our troubles on this trip were not over. We still had Bearvalley ahead of us, and there had been a lot of snow fall, as we found out when we got up into upper Bearvalley. I was driving along serenely on top of the snow when without warning [the horses,]Dick and Brownie broke through the snow in a ravine and went in all over. I just had to get out and shovel all the snow out to the ground under the wagon, around the horses and in front of them for 20 or so yards to get out.

After shoveling a while a stranger rode up on horseback and asked if he could help. I offered him the shovel, saying I was about spent. But he refused it for fear of getting his feet wet. He said his horse was good to pull by the horn of the saddle, but I called his attention to the uselessness of such an effort and told him my other team was good to pull, too, but it would be impossible to drag the wagon through the snow bank. So he rode off.

I finally got the road cleared, but it took so long that we had to camp at the upper ranch instead of going on to Paragoonah and staying with Annie's sister, Hannah, as we had hoped to do. We stopped at the ranch house and I made a good fire in the fireplace, and brought in the grub box, then hitched Dick and Brownie on the buggy and pulled it to the top of the summit. Annie was almost in tears when I returned. I was not worried at the time, but have often wondered what Annie would or could have done had something happened to me and the team here or [while] bringing the buggy over the Escalante mountains.

She could have gotten away from camp at the foot of Escalante Mountain with either a2 horses, as the wagon road (?) was broken there, but I had all the horses. The small team she had at Bearvalley couldn't have moved the wagon from there as it took the four to pull the wagon to the top of the summit the next morning. I was afraid of more snow break-through like the one in upper Bear valley, because I knew what caused that was the ground warming up for spring under the snow and softening the snow on the underside.

But I guess the snow wasn't quite deep enough any other place in the road for this to happen. The snow that did bread through was six feet deep. When we passed the measuring stake on the Escalante Mountain, I noticed the snow was up to the 110 inch line. I have never been in either place with a team since. I have been in Escalante and through Bearvalley both by auto but both roads are changed.

We made Paragoonah the first day from Bearvalley and spent the night and possibly the next day with Annie's sister Hannah Robinson. The balance of the trip was without incident. But we were glad to be home again.

Neither have I told of an experience Will and I had the next year after we left Escalante. Father went out in the Burnt Canyon area north of Spring valley, Nevada, to herd sheep for Hyde Bros. of Murray, Utah, and Will and I went out to see him and I thought Will would stay and let Father come home, but Will came back with me. The night we reached the ranch at Burnt Canyon, Father wasn't there so we just turned our horses in the lot and shut the gate, but had no place to sleep as there was just the dirt floor in the old log cabin and the ground was wet. We built up a big fire in the fireplace and pulled two small tables up close to it and slept on the tables with our saddles under our heads and our saddle blankets for cover.

We had nothing to eat, neither did we sleep much as it was high up in the mountains, early summer and turned cold before morning. The horses fared well, though, as the grass was good in the lot. Wen daylight came we found a note Pa had left for us, which directed us to his camp. We got there about 7:30 a.m. and found a camp breakfast very satisfying.

I didn't know until years afterward why Will didn't stay and relieve my father, then he told me why. We saw lion tracks everywhere and heard them roar at night, and he was afraid of lions, which stemmed from another experience he and I had. As I say elsewhere, we traded our farm in Escalante for sheep and Will and I were left with them for the summer. We caught a lion in a trap and it looked like it was caught by only two toes and could get loose any minute and kill us. Wills first shot just cut the bridge of its nose and made it ferocious.

His fear of its getting loose unnerved him so badly that he couldn't even hit the lion. My Father and brother, Ed, were building some fence about a mile below our camp and when they heard the shooting Pa sent Ed on a horse to investigate. So Will sent Ed back for Pa to come up and kill the lion, which he did. We found then that it couldn't get out of the trap as it was caught in a #4 bear trap with teeth on the jaws and three of these were through the foot above the toes. But Will never lost his fear of lions. I didn't think he was afraid of anything! This lion measured nine feet from tip to tip.

I see I haven't told of my experience with the pigs and the dry farmers. I went down to my ranch one day in November or December and found two pigs I had left there had gotten into my stock-yard and were destroying the corn. So I decided to take them to Enterprise. I made a lid for the wagon box out of the door to the cow stable and drove the wagon with the rear wheels in a gutter. Put the pig trough in and coaxed the pigs in, using the horse's stable door for a ramp. But when I attempted to drop the rear end gate I made a little noise that startled the largest pig and he dodged out. I tried to coax him back in but couldn't so decided to rope him and lead him in. As soon as I got the rope on him, he got mad and started to fight. Just then, I saw some [men with] teams headed to-ward Enterprise, northeast of the ranch, so [I] jumped on my saddle horse and run over and stopped them and asked them to come and help me load the pig. But they refused, so I went back and drove the wagon into the corral which was built on a hill, let the hind wheels down in holes, put the stable door up for a ramp again, tied the pig up in the rope by wrapping it round and round him, and rolled him into the wagon.

Then I got a few things out of the house and took off. About two miles out I found those [same men and their] two hay teams, the lead one stuck in the mud in the ditch. I looked the situation over, had him take his team off and hitched mine on and pulled his wagon out. The other one admitted his team wasn't reliable, so I pulled his wagon across [the ditch] also. You should have heard these men apologize then for not helping me with the pig. Told them if they had helped me with the pig I wouldn't have been there to pull them across the ditch. But they maintained it was the "judgement of God" on them for refusing to help me. The big pig dressed 195 lbs., two weeks later.

I had a summer experience when working on the Zion's Park lodge about 1931 or -32. It rained one Saturday afternoon and my old Model T was too close to the lodge so water run off the roof onto the car and wet my coils. When we quit that night it refused to start. Another man was having trouble starting his car a short distance away so I went and helped him [get] his car started, then said I would tie a big rope to the front of mine and get him to pull me a couple of rods and mine would start. He said, "O.K.", [then] drove to the Bowser [?] and got some gas and took off for home. Wilford Bleak came and took the coils out of my car and said we would go down and put them in the range oven while we ate, then it would start. He and Noăne [or Hoăne] finished supper ahead of me, got my key and took the coils and when I had finished my supper they were back with my car.

When I got in to go, Will[ford] said, "You'll find that "bird" stuck down about Springdale and when you do, just drive out around him and go on". Sure enough, I found him in the lane at Springdale, and [so I] hitched onto him and got his car going again. It was raining a little again, and [since I was following him] I had this same thing to do every few miles. I pulled him out of Toquerville and went on ahead for the first time. I had only gotten up the hill a little when my light wires seemed to short and the lights went out. I got out to check the trouble and the other man passed me and went on, but before I got to Leeds I caught up with this man [who was] stopped again with a flat tire.

He had no patches, so I got some out of my car and fixed his tube and helped him get going again. I pulled him up onto the Harrisburg bench and up on the Washington Black ridge. When we got here he said he was too tired to go any farther, so I gave him some candy bars I had and drove on. It was nearly two o'clock a.m. when I got home. Dick Morgan was riding with him to the foot of the Laverkin Hill. He lived in Hurricane. When I got to the lodge Monday morning I found that Dick had beat me back and told of his experience of the Saturday night and some one who rode with me, probably Jess Pearce, had told the rest of it. Anyway, the man treated this man so coolly that he quit.

Every one on the job, nearly, called me "Bishop", the name a carpenter had [once] called me in derision on the rail road in Nevada between Rocks and Los Vegas a year or so before when we were replacing the old wood bridges with concrete ones. This man had married a Mormon bishop's daughter in Salt Lake, and I guess didn't live to suit his father-in-law, and he was jealous of me because I had had first-aid training, the only man on the job who had some. I had used it several times to relieve the suffering of men who had got hurt on the job. [I also] entertained the men a lot at night by playing the guitar and singing for them thus getting the good will of not only the men but the contractor and his foreman as well. And, too, I refused to drink coffee at noon on the job or in camp. The name "Bishop" was the worst he could think of evidently, so he called me "Bishop".

Albert Lang and Hale Pearce were working on [that] railroad job and also at Zion's Park lodge so I suppose it was them that started the custom up there. Lionel Chidester from Panguitch was my carpenter helper, and Dick Morgan's job was to keep us in lumber, nails, etc. and to keep all waste scraps out of our way. He called me "Bishop" like the others did, and Chidester and I called him "Brother Morgan" or President Morgan". He didn't like it and said he didn't want to be called "Brother" by such hypocrites as Chidester and I. But after this experience the first time I called him "Brother Morgan", being Welsh, he said, "Brother 'all, I consider it a Honor to be called brother by a man like you.

Writing about the railroad job reminds me that I learned to fabricate reinforcing steel on this job. There was not enough of this class of work to justify keeping fabricators on the job so Schraven, the Contractor, arranged with the union to let the carpenters do it. Monrad Monson knew how to do it and taught the rest of us how. I became an expert at it. Monson being the only man on the job who could do it faster, and only because he was a lot taller and had better reach than I did.

He could stand on the ground and nail lumber on the forms as high as I could reach from a saw horse. This knowledge was useful when we built the Bank of Southern Utah building, in Cedar City, as I was the only one there who knew how to do it, so was put in charge of this work.

I also learned how to do dry finishing with sheet rock in Nevada by necessity. The only plasterer in Lincoln County, Nevada, left and I had to turn to dry finishing and became an expert at it. Had Leon Jennings known this when we remodeled the old Joe Snow Building for Bill McMullin, someone else may have gotten his neck broke instead of me.[!]

I wish to say here, that I have worked under some fine bosses. John Schraven, Contractor on that railroad job was a nice old man, and his foreman, Bill Hatton of Provo, Utah, was the kindest man I ever worked for. In the five months I worked on the railroad bridge job I never heard him speak a cross word to anybody. If a man didn't do an honest days work, Hatton just gave him his check the next morning at breakfast.

Hy Kuntz, whom I worked under at Zion's Park lodge and Cedar Breaks was very considerate, and Mr. Anderson from northern Utah was nice to work for on the Bank of Southern Utah building. I found Albert E. Miller of St. George a very good man to work for, and so was Thomas Dixon and Carol Miller of Caliente, Nevada, and a lot of others. Even Ora Thompson, who called me "Bishop" in derision became friendly to me after I had rendered first aid to a special friend of his who got a big toe split on the railroad. I washed this man's foot in a disinfectant and dressed it every night and morning for about two weeks.

I haven't told of carrying two sharp packet knives, one in my hand and the other in my teeth, as I crawled through a thick, patch of Manzanita that was supposed to be infested with bears and which I was forbidden to go through between South Creek and Sweet Water on the East Fork of the Sevier River, the year we left Escalante. I have often wondered what would have happened had I come up with a bear or two on one of these trips.

I think before I close this history, I should say something about our children. We had four girls born to us. The last one, Linda [Malinda], died of summer complaint in Washington in her second year. We had been married a little over seven years when the oldest girl, Grace, was born. As she grew up she took naturally to ranch life, and was a great help to me on the farm. We started to give her organ lessons when she was about ten years old. I drove my old Model T Ford from Washington to St. George and got the teacher, Lucile Cottam, and took her to my home for the lessons then brought her back again, once a week.

We soon learned we were trying to make an organist or pianist of the wrong girl, so switched the lessons to Priscilla. Grace, however, kept up the study and is a fairly good pianist, now. She married Jack C. Reid who was born and raised at Hinkley, Utah. They live in Bell Gardens, California. He is a very able carpenter and concrete finisher and is kept busy most of the time. I worked with him several years ago on finishing work for two contractors in Los Angeles, and for a while in January, 1956, on remodeling the chapel of the Grant Ward in the South Los Angeles Stake at Bell Gardens. Jack had supervision of this work.

Grace is very active in the LDS church down there, especially Primary, Sunday school, Relief Society, and in PTA work. She is a good housekeeper and a good mother. Has seven children, five boys and two girls. The oldest boy, David, is now filling a mission in the Western States Mission, and was at Albuquerque, New Mexico when we had the last letter from him. We send Grace ten dollars each month to help him in his mission. Jack is also active in the church.

Priscilla married Whitney A. Cude, a convert to the L.D.S Church from Texas. He was born at or near Dallas, Texas. He is an expert electrician. A graduate of the Coyne School, of Northwestern University mathematics and electric departments, and of a school at Tacoma, Washington. The government sent him to the last two institutions during World War II to prepare him for Fire Control 1st Class, which position he held in the navy during World War II on the light cruiser, St. Louis.

I worked with him both before and after the war. He taught me plumbing and house wiring, and I did a lot of this work in Nevada. He also taught me a lot of higher mathematics, such as differential equations, advanced trigonometry, graphs and logerisms [logarithms], six point logerisms, calcus [calculus], etc. He is currently stationed with a naval force with the rank of Chief, in Korea.

Priscilla is a professional pianist, the last lessons I paid for her cost me $5.00 per lesson, under either Charles or Arthur Sheppard in Los Angeles. She later studied under Eddie Duchen and others. She plays piano for a big dancing school and piano in one of the leading dance orchestras in Portland, Oregon. She has done some composing that has merit, and had done a lot of arranging popular songs for their orchestra. She has served a great deal in piano work and conducting in both ward and stake levels, especially in Portland, Oregon, where she lives.

She also teaches a lot, especially in primary and M.I.A. She has three children, two girls and a boy. The oldest one, Dallas, is married and has three children, all girls. Priscilla is a good housekeeper and manager and better driver than most women.

Desma, our youngest girl, also married a convert to the church. Floyd L. Galway came to Panaca from Indiana with the C.C.C. boys. He was more steady than the other boys in the camp, didn't smoke or drink nor chase around. He was interested in watch-making and usually had a few clocks and watches in his room for cleaning, repairing or adjusting for people of the town and, or, his buddies in the camp. I did a lot of carpentry work in the camp and the foreman usually assigned me one of the boys as a helper. One day he assigned Floyd to help me build an oil house and I liked him and asked for him after that.

Floyd began investigating Mormonism and started attending Sunday school. Sometimes I took him home to Sunday dinner and then back to sacrament meeting. I was an officer of the Sunday school and ward clerk. When Desma came home from school from Provo, Utah, for the summer vacation, I took Floyd to dinner and introduced them. They began going together, but before Desma went back to school, they broke up.

When the C.C. camp was closed Floyd went north and got a job on the Deer Creek Reservoir. He stayed at Provo and went to S[unday] school there and happened to go to the same ward Desma was in. They renewed their acquaintance, and before spring were married. After their marriage, Floyd opened a watch repair shop in Fillmore but soon learned he needed more training, so soon after, they went to Marion, Indiana, where Desma got a job as credit manager for Sears Roebuck & Co. and Floyd went to Elgin, Illinois, and entered the Elgin watch-making school. After graduating, he remained there a while as inspector, then they returned to Utah.

Desma is a good bookkeeper and kept books for the Caliente Rapid Transfer Co., at Caliente, Nevada, the last year she was home. She also served as credit manager for Sears, Roebuck & Co. in their Sugar House store in Salt Lake City. But the thing she majored in and is best fitted for educationally is botany. Prof. Vasco M. Tanner told me she was the best botanist in the west. She had charge of the herbarium at B.Y.U. and rearranged it and reclassified all the specimens in it as well as classifying new specimens sent in by former students from all over the world where they were stationed in the service.

She taught agronomy one or two terms while Dr. Martin was away on leave, studying. She has four children - a girl and three boys. Floyd is now employed bye the Yale Lock Co. as Time Lock Inspector for Utah, Idaho, Colorado and New Mexico. He travels most of the time. Desma also held the position of seed analyst for Utah for a term in Salt Lake City. She also is a good housekeeper and manager.

I know I have failed to tell half the things I have done. I have broken wild cows to milk and wild horses to work and ride, have worked in mines enough to be a good miner and was called the "best judge of gold, silver and lead ore" in Lincoln County, Nevada. I haven't told of how I discovered a mistake in the grade plans of the power plant at Gunlock and of how, at the same time the men [working] on the ditch to this plant discovered a mistake in the ditch grade, and how I recommended Bob Kenworthy for the engineers job as I was probably the only man in Dixie who knew Bob was a graduate Civil Engineer.

Bob was given the job and made good at it insomuch that he has worked at this profession ever since. He supported me in my contention that the grade plans of the plant were wrong and that I would have to add three feet to the height of my foundation forms to bring the plant high enough so the water would run from the turbine pit into the creek, and not from the creek into the turbine pit [!].

I have not told of setting ratchet and offbearing [shoulder carrying] at a saw mill, nor of offbearing [at] brick yards and of helping build brick kilns and burn the brick; nor of filling lime kilns with lime and rock and helping burn the lime.

Probably a lot of other things will have to be added to this history after I read the printed or typewritten copy.

I have even forgotten to mention that my daughter, Desma, lives at 2246 Windsor St. in Salt Lake City, with her children and husband when he is home.

I find I haven't said a word about my experiences as a veterinarian. I was meteorological observer for the government at Lund, Utah, and the man in charge of these stations knew I had a ranch near Enterprise so he sent me two books, one on diseases of cattle, and the other on the diseases of horses. I realized the need of someone in the country who knew something about these things so began to study them intensely. After about five years of study and observation I began to practice just in a neighborly way.

I went to Eldredge's ranch in the New Castle project one day and found one of their purebred Percheron mares down and couldn't get up. I surmised azoturia [?] right at once, and told glen just how it happened. He said I was right but that a veterinarian who had been there pronounced it lung fever. I maintained she had no symptoms of lung fever and there were no conditions to cause it, but there was a natural set up here for azotura [?]. I told him lung fever was brought on by an animal being exposed to drafts or cold rain when tired and resembled pneumonia in humans, but that azoturia was caused by a horse being fed on high protein feed and not used for a while, and then suddenly exercised violently which caused the reserve protein stored in the loins to change to a poison that stagnated the blood and caused the horse to break down in the coupling and fall.

He said they had been keeping the horses in the yard which was too small for exercise and feeding then all the alfalfa hay and oats they would eat, then one day some of them got out and a dog chased them out into the field and that three of them fell while running from the dog. All three of these died. A few days later, this one got out and the dog chased her until she fell. He couldn't get her up so loaded her on a drag and pulled her into the barn with a truck.

I asked him if there was any olive oil and ammonia in the house. He went to see and brought back a bottle of each, then got an empty bottle to mix them in. I mixed some liniment for him of these and showed him how to use it. In a few days, he had her on her feet and she fully recovered. A week later their Kentucky Saddle Stallion got out, was chased by the same dog with the same results. He came for me in his car and treated the horse and helped get him into shelter and he soon recovered.

I also saved a valuable work horse for Aaron Huntsman and several horses being pastured by my brother one fall when they were chased in an effort to corral them. I saved quite a few cows at Enterprise that had distention of he rumen. This was the old imaginary disease of "loss of quid" or "cud", which ever way you want to spell it. I've seen men hunt all over the corral for a cow's 'cud' when she had distention of the rumen [?]. When it couldn't be found they would say she had swallowed it and couldn't belch it up, so they would get a greasy sour dish rag and force it down her throat with a broom handle to make the cow belch her cud up.

Sometimes this worked as the retching of the cow would start the clogged food in her first stomach to breaking up so she could bring it up and chew it again. A cow or any ruminant has several stomachs and the food they eat is chewed but very little at first and goes down into the first stomach. Later it is belched up and chewed finer and goes down into another stomach. Sometimes if the food is too coarse and dry and the cow doesn't have enough water this food packs and clogs together and can't be brought up and chewed again. This gave rise to the old idea of loss of cud. In this case, the thing to do is go into the hollow of her side, on the left side outside her body, and knead and work at this mass with the fists and break it up so she can bring it up in small amounts to chew it again.

To drench her with water with a little corn syrup or molasses in it helps. We diagnose this trouble by pressing on the cows left side, in the hollow in front of the hip with the finger tips. If it feels like stiff dough and the finger prints remain for a short time, the trouble is almost surely distention of the rumen. Sometimes cows with this will grunt when they walk, and sometimes paw and bawl with a deep tone, which is sometimes mistaken for rabies.

Two other imaginary diseases were "wolf in the tail" and "hollow horn". I have seen men split the skin on the underside of the end of a cows tail and rub salt in it to cure "wolf in the tail", and throw a cow and bore a hole in the horn about two inches from the head and pour turpentine in to cure "hollow horn". All the first cow needed was the grubs pressed out of her back, and the grub holes treated with a little cobalt in her feed. When the hair falls away from a cows horns it indicates a shortage of cobalt in the feed.

I saved a lot of good cows and horses in Enterprise and continued the practice when I came to Dixie [St. George area]. There was no veterinarian in the county then, and John T. Woodbury and I served as substitutes. The college had a hypodermic syringe, needles and anti-toxin for hemoragic septicemia [?] in a locker in the hall and John T. and I each had a key to it. This disease was very prevalent at that time, having been brought in with dairy cattle purchased in the central states. When cows became sick the owner contacted which ever one of us was easiest to reach, and either of us would get the material from the college locker and go treat the cows if it was hemoragic septicemia [?], clean and return the hypo to the locker.

I also took warts out of cows ears, which made them mean and brindle, and had a liniment that would remove splints, curbs, side bones, bone spavin and, if used in time, would cure ringbone. It would take any bone or gristle growth off a horse anywhere. The liniment was also good for sprains and strained tendons, on either man or beast and if camphor gum was added it provided relief from rheumatic pains and arthritis. I still keep the liniment in the house.

After I went to Panaca, Nevada, I continued this practice there. I had only one case of hemoragic septicemia there, and that was my own cow that my brother took to Kanarra [?] from here when she was a calf. I couldn't find the anti-toxin out there, so saved my own cow with watermelons. I cured several cows of mastitis, though, and saved several from alkali poisoning, and some from poison by hydrocyanic acid that was deposited on arrow grass seed heads. One of the best remedies I found for this was cotton seed cake. The oil counteracted the acid. Here, too, I saved horses from azoturia.

A vet that was brought in from the outside was as wrong on this as was the one at New Castle years before. He diagnosed the trouble as brain fever, and was treating the horses for that. I saved every horse buy one. Sometimes, horses lay down with brain fever and seem to be afraid to get up but can. Brain fever is caused by the bite of a small fly that resembles a deer fly, but they are only carriers and can give the disease only after biting another animal that has it. These books have been worth a lot of money to me and my friends.

I also took three prospectors courses at Panaca and learned to use a blowpipe and platinum wire in the identification of minerals, as well as the chemical tests for these. I later bought a course in mineralogy and a complete [kit] for testing ores. I can test for any mineral and a lot of the elements in the earth's crust, and have done a lot of this work. The tests for lead, vanadium, copper, mercury and silver are quite simple. The others are more or less complicated, some of them very much so. For an example, only two chemicals are used to test lead, and I keep them on hand mixed and ready all the time and can make a positive test for lead anytime in three minutes or less.

I started to take a machinists course at Panaca, but didn't get to finish it because of a government ruling, that to be eligible for the course one had to be able to go any place the government wanted to send them with an hour's notice after completing the course. Only one man in the group could do this, so the course was discontinued. However, I did learn to use the lathes, threading machines and jointer in the month or six weeks the course ran, and have some small tools I made to show for it. In fact I got good enough at it to make a shaft for the water pump when the shaft broke and I had to have another one the next day to pump our school culinary water supply tank full of water before our water turn was out.

This shaft had to be lathed to a different diameter on each end with S.A.E thread on one end and standard 13 pitch thread on the other. And the center had to have a seat for a half moon key. This was the hardest thing to do, as there was no bit for the jointer narrow enough to cut it nor anything to make one of. I clamped the shaft to the table of the drill press and bored three holes in it at different depths, and cut out extra material by hand with a small cold chisel. This shaft was still in use in the pump three years later. I was caretaker at the Lincoln County High School at the time. As a result of taking this course I was good enough at the work to be offered the position of machinists helper with Dan Webster in the Union Pacific shops at Caliente. Webster wanted me but the shop foreman had promised the position to one of his own personal friends.

An old German miner by the name of Weber, as I remember it, taught me how to sharpen picks and temper steel when I was about 14 years old. He had taken a contract to drive two tunnels on the old Hebron ditch in the mouth of the canyon on your right going to the Enterprise Reservoir, and the company was to "muck out" for him. Uncle George Holt, president of the company, sent me over to wheel the waste out for Weber in a wheelbarrow. A strong friendship developed between us, and he taught me how to do these things. He played a violin, but had none with him, so I had him come to my home and play mine and eat with us occasionally. He went to DeLamas from there and I believe was the first presiding elder for the L.D.S. Church over the DeLamas branch. He was a convert to the church from Germany.

The Catholic Priest mentioned under the subject, "Work" [see part 6], was a Zumstein [?], whose parents lived in Caliente [, Nevada]. I was quite well acquainted with his brothers Andy and John, who run garages in Caliente. I attended the funeral of Angelo Clark in Pioche a few days before this incident happened, and the Rev. Zumstein preached the funeral sermon. I was surprised to hear him quote copiously from the Book of Mormon. He would just say "It is recorded in scripture" or "one of the prophets said", and then quote [it]. In house-to-house canvassing for the Utah Woolen Mills in Caliente, I came to his home. He at first refused to let me in, then changed his mind when I smiled at him and [he] opened the door and bade me enter. I recognized him at once as the minister that spoke at the Clarks funeral and made some comment about his quoting from the Book of Mormon.

Then he showed me his Book of Mormon, underscored from cover to cover with different color ink, each color, he said, indicates a subject. He then showed me this palimpsest [a parchment that had been erased for other use] and said this had converted him to Mormonism, and that he was going to Salt Lake [City] in about a month and would be baptized while there. He said he had watched for years to see if the Prophet Joseph Smith had ever given the name of the Brother of Jared, then one day found it in a magazine published years ago by the Primary Association. In this article the prophet walks down the street in Nauvoo, and stops to talk with Caleb Cahoon. Bro. Cahoon invites him in to bless and name his newborn son. The prophet doesn't ask what name to give the baby, but blesses him and gives him the name of Mahonri Moriancumer. Bro. Cahoon asked where he got the name, and he said it was the name of the Brother of Jared. The Rev. Zumstein said that was the name given for him on this palimpsest. I asked him how he would make a living if he joined the church and he showed me the type-written manuscript of a History of the Bible he had written, and said when he went to Salt Lake and joined the church, he would have this published in book form, and that the revenue from the sale of the books would take care of him nicely. He also told me that as a Catholic Priest, he had access to information that no other writer of a history of the bible had access to, so he knew this was the best history of the bible ever written.

He had a few extra sheets of a few pages of this manuscript, which he gave me. When [I and my family later] left St. George, I had put these sheets in a small box upstairs under my journal I kept in the mission field and a few musical compositions of mine and some other papers. Desma thought the contents were valueless, so burned them up.

Mr. Zumstein told me he wanted to go on a mission back to his native country, and expected to devote his life to the work of the L.D.S Church. He told me that a monk in Armenia gave him the palimpsest when he toured the holy land after graduating from the Catholic school for ministers. He was killed in an automobile acci-dent about a week later, so he had no chance to join the church as he had planned. I got the necessary information from his father for Apostle Ballard, who requested me to do so to have his temple work done, and Apostle Ballard took care of it in the Salt Lake Temple. I asked Andy [his brother] one day what became of his history of the bible and he said that as soon as his brother was killed the Catholic

Authorities locked his house, which was Catholic property, and that all they brought to his mother was a few personal affects of his brother. [He] said he asked about the Book of Mormon and this bible history and was told it was none of his business what became of them, as they were Catholic property.

[Ref.: Page 29 in this history]

I just mention getting stuck in the mud in Bearvalley [Utah] when I turned out for a load of lumber, but don't say why I was there nor where I was going. I also mention the fact that the wife of the bishop's second counselor had cancer of the stomach. This last was the reason for me being here. I was out to Hatch finishing a home for Sam Barnhurst that I had built the year before. One day this woman, Priscilla Riggs, who was my wife's aunt and the woman who partly raised her as she was an orphan at 14, sent for me and said the doctor said she couldn't live more than a month, and said she wanted to see Annie [my wife] before she died.

I was on my way to Enterprise to get my wife when this incident happened [i.e. getting stuck in the mud]. When we got back to Hatch Uncle Will R. Riggs had taken Priscilla to Loa [Utah] to be treated by Dr. Elias Blackburn, who had been blessed by Apostle Amasa Lyman to heal cancer. When they returned a month later Aunt Priscilla was setting in the spring seat in the wagon driving the teams. Dr. Blackburn cured cancer by administering to them by the power of the priesthood. He sent word to have two elders called for a week at a time to anoint the roots of the cancer with oil every night just at sundown, and every morning at son up and command these roots to wither up and die in the name of the Lord and by the power of the priesthood.

I was called with an other elder to officiate the first week. We could feel the roots of the cancer, as large as my finger, two going up over her shoulders, four around her body to the spine in her back and two going down to below her knees. We could feel these getting smaller each day, and when I and the other elders was called back for our second term about three weeks or a month later they were practically gone -- and disappeared entirely that week. About two years later she gave birth to a baby who grew into a fine man and she outlived her husband.

Two other faith promoting incidents in my life I am overlooking: One concerns my fathers return from Burnt Canyon where Will and I went to visit him. we got a letter from him about the first of August saying he would leave for home on a certain day and would get home about five days later, as he would probably have to walk all the way. He should have reached home the day we got the letter, but didn't come that day nor the next. The next morning. I went down in the field to change the water and when I got that done I climbed up on the hill below the field to where I could see down the road in hopes I would see him coming.

When I didn't, I kneeled down and with all the trust of a boy asked my Heavenly Father to send him safely home to us. Every day after this, at about the same time, I climbed to the same place and watched for him to come. On the fifth day I was rewarded by seeing my father coming. After the usual greetings at the house, mother asked why he was so long coming. Then he explained that Mr. Hyde was 4 or 5 days late coming, and when he did come he didn't bring a relief man.

They talked it over and father agreed to stay two or three weeks longer. Mr. Hyde started home the next morning, but in about half an hour came back and said, "Brother Hall, I feel impressed to stay here and let you go home, so while you get your things together I will write a letter to my partner to send out a man on horseback to take my place and you can post the letter at the first post office you get to on your way out".   I know why Brother Hyde got this "impression" to send my father home. There was a boy on his knees praying 150 miles away with all the simple faith of a boy that couldn't be denied.

The other incident [later in my life] concerns a grade Jersey Heifer I was taking care of for Israel Barlow Jr. of Salt Lake City. I got a letter from brother Barlow one day, about two years before [this], asking me to go to the New Castle Reclamation Co.'s farm north of the town of New Castle and get a cow and a six-months old calf of his that were at this farm. He said [in his letter] the bank of Beaver had attached the company's cattle, or intended to do so, and that these animals of his had the company mark and brand on [them] and would be taken by the bank unless he got them away.

I therefore went and got them and took them to my ranch and put my mark and brand on them according to his instructions. The next spring the cow gave birth to a heifer calf sired by a Jersey bull. The other calf was turned over to Glen Eldredge who butchered it and sent it up to Mr. Barlow with others he was sending to his father. This heifer calf is the one now under discussion at this time. I had another letter from Mr. Barlow asking me to take this heifer down to Glen Eldredge so he could ship her up to him with some he was shipping up to his father, saying if I would do this I could have the cow [as payment] for this and my other trouble and care of the animals. The letter also said Glen was shipping the next Wednesday. I got the letter Monday about four o'clock p.m. and the heifer was out on the range with my other cattle.

The next morning I got up early and got my chores done and after breakfast saddled Brownie and started out to find this animal. I thought if I could find her in this one day I could start for Modena with her the next morning and meet Glen's bunch somewhere on the way. I rode up onto the Onion Hill and looked the country over. To the west was Willow Spring country and sweeping to the south was the Hogs Back Range and Enterprise Reservoir area. And east from this area was the Little Reservoir area and the north and west sides of Flat Top Mountain, in all a 20 x 6 mile area, covered with thick scrub oak and service berry, growing so thick in places that one could pass within twenty yards of a cow and never see her.

How could one man find a certain animal in that area in one day alone. I need help. So I rode down to a clump of cedar trees and got off my horse, and went into the trees and got down on my knees and laid my difficulty before the Lord and asked for help. [Afterwards] I rode down to Arthur Barlocker's field, and instead of going west from his N. W. corner to Willow Springs as I had intended to, I turned my horse south and rode down to the creek and there was the heifer feeding in the creek bottom.

When I got Back to my ranch with her I had only been gone about an hour. I rode to the house and told Annie of my good fortune and went on with the heifer, arriving at Eldredge's farm in time for lunch at 12:30. And after resting and visiting a while, went back home. I doubt very much if I could have gotten this heifer at all if my Father [in Heaven] hadn't answered my prayer in the affirmative.

One accomplishment of my boyhood I have overlooked. That of marble playing. I was champion knuckle buster marble player of Escalante when I was twelve years old. None of the boys of my age would play with me for keeps and I could hold my own with most of the boys two or three years older than I. In fact I only remember one boy older than I that could beat me and play fair, and that was Arlo Griffen, and he was about six years my senior. I remember breaking Zetland Mitchell one Saturday morning in front of the co-op store. We met there early and he challenged me to a game for keeps to run one hour or until one of us was broke, with an hour limit.

We made the ring, about three-and-a-half or four feet in diameter and rolled the first shot. You rolled your taw [or shooter marble] across the ring and the one whose marble stopped closest to the line on the opposite side had the first shot. I got my first shot and won all his marbles without him getting a shot. I felt sorry for him because he was game enough to sit and roll all his marbles into the ring, including his "taw" and never get a shot. I gave him back his taw and one or two other marbles.

We never played for keeps again, but did play some for fun when no one else would play with either of us. If a boy we didn't know wanted to play for keeps we always looked at the back of his shooting hand and if the knuckle of the middle finger was sore or had a scab on it, we wouldn't play with him, as this was evidence that he cheated by "fudging", shoving his hand up against the marbles when he shot. I have noticed that some men go all through life with a sore knuckle.

It was at Escalante, when I was eight years old that my uncle Rob and Dave Miller took me and secretly taught me how to ride race horses. I was to be their jockey. But before the big spring races started my father found out about it and put his foot down on it definitely. I rode lots of horses in races run for fun, but only rode one race that had any money up on it, that I knew of. This one was at Modena after I was married, in fact it was two or three years after Grace was born. One of the big circuses had advertised that they would hold a regular circus in Modena on a certain day and I would guess that a thousand people had come from the surrounding country to see it.

After these notices were sent out a transportation workers strike was called on the R.R. just the night before the circus was to leave Milford, which tied them up in Milford. It is only natural for that many people to stage some kind of a celebration of their own, so contests of all kinds were entered into. Horse pulling matches both work and saddle horses, boxing matches, jumping, foot racing, etc., and finally horse racing. Andrew Price of St. George had left his sorrel race horse in Modena a few days before when he went to Salt Lake, and Bert [?] got this horse out and was showing him to the crowd. Israel Adair had a black horse aver there that he got at Kanab or Orderville that was race stock.

Of course these horses were finally matched for a race. When the horses run the sorrel horse was ahead about two lengths, and I noticed that the boy riding the black was sitting straight up, thereby catching a lot of wind pressure, was whipping and kicking the horse and had his reins absolutely loose. I remarked that the black horse was the fastest if they would let me ride him, so his backers doubled the bet and I rode the horse in the second race. I just crouched down on the horse and held my reins tight and beat the sorrel about three lengths [of] "open daylight". The same man rode the sorrel horse in both races. My wife and her cousin criticized me quite severely for riding this race when I knew money was bet on it, and I have never rode one since if I knew money was up on it.

I did quite a lot of foot racing and some jumping, too. When I worked in the store for B.J. Lund & Co. in Modena. I was beat only once in a foot race, and that when I had been almost on the run in the store for two or three days during a lay off in [sheep] shearing because of rain. I didn't want to run and others insisted on the race, saying I had beaten this boy's brother, Jewett Woods, a little while before, and they were sure Jewett was faster than Adlae. They were wrong, but we didn't know it at the time.

Another thing we didn't know was that the man who acted as starter of the race was betting on Adlae. This man was a sheep shearer from Idaho, who had been a high school coach in Idaho. We learned after the race that he had slipped some money to a friend to bet on Woods. He favored Woods on the start by allowing him to break the line ahead of the gun and not calling him back. He was ten feet off the line when the gun crashed and I couldn't catch him.

Lou Lund offered to bet $500 that I could beat Woods on a 100 yard race in a month, but I had gained on Woods and his backers were afraid. Woods was herding sheep for Joe Prince and was in prime condition, as Joe had massaged his legs and rubbed him down every day. All the training I had was running up and down the cellar steps, carrying canned goods, etc., up to fill the store shelves every day. Lou was sure I would be ten to twenty feet faster if I was massaged and had a rub down every day.

Among other men I beat in Modena in the running broad jump was Willie Thornton of Parowan. Willie had won the State High School meet in Salt Lake about a week before I beat him in Modena. In this match he jumped 21 feet 2 inches and I jumped 21 feet, 8 inches. Joe Prince thought this beat Sherm Cooper's record made in 1913, but when he got Sherm's record [out, he found] he had jumped 22 feet, 4 inches. Lou thought it was 21-4. Few men have jumped closer to Sherm Cooper's record than I did that day at Modena.

Some one lost $50 on this match, and I won a lot of money for Lou Lund and others in Modena, but this all happened several years before I rode the black horse in Modena, and promised I would never ride another race on which money was bet, if I knew it was. This promise stemmed from something I said when speaking in sacrament meeting in Enterprise a short time before. In my remarks I said a man believed what he did and not what he said he believed. I also said I didn't believe in gambling.

Annie and her cousin, Sadie, put it up to me this way: Did I believe it wrong to gamble, or did I believe it was all right, so rode the horse? Did I believe what I said I believed or did I believe what my act confirmed? Anyway, I have never rode a race, nor run nor jumped since where I even thought that money was being bet on the outcome.

In the running broad jump, form has lot to do with it. When I jumped I threw my feet forward and assumed almost a horizontal position in the air and just before my heels touched the ground I gave my body a flip that shoved my feet a little farther forward and when the heels touched ground my body was coming up, so instead of sliding and landing finally on my back, I just trotted off.

I speak elsewhere of herding, shearing, and dipping sheep, well, in the fall about 1911, I got a letter from Will Lund asking me to get a crew of men and come to Modena and take charge of the dipping vats and dip sheep that fall. I got my brothers Will, Ed, Rob, Jim, and possibly Harold, and Ivor Clove and went over to Modena and took charge of the dipping that fall. I put my brother Will in charge of the furnace and I had the responsibility of Mixing the dip. Will and I would go to the plant at daylight and while the vat was filling with water he would fire up the furnace and I would mix the dip. While we were doing this the other boys would get breakfast, as we were camped near the stockyards where the dipping plant was located, and "Batching".

When breakfast was over the dip would be hot enough to go to work. We started early and worked late as we were dipping for [a price of] so much per thousand sheep. This job was like Abe Church of Caliente said about a cement mixer. He was running a wheelbarrow wheeling concrete up on a floor about 3-1/2 feet above ground and dumping it into the basement forms. He was a little fellow, about 125 pounds, and I offered to have one of the other boys change with him. "No," He said, "There is no snap around a cement mixer".

There is no snap around a dipping vat, either. Sheep can't be driven through a vat. One has to catch them, one at a time and throw them in. A small pen for this purpose is built right against the vat. Two men work in this pen, throwing the sheep in the vat. Will and Jim worked in this pen, at a little extra pay. When two men catch and throw 8,000 sheep into this vat in one day, they are tired. This was our average day's run. We dipped 240,000 head of sheep in 30 days. There is another pen about the same size adjoining this one. The job of Ed and Harold, if he was with us, and the herder was to keep this auxiliary pen full of sheep. Rob ducked the sheep under in the vat.

I worked where the sheep started up a chute out of the vat. About every third sheep on an average has to be pulled out of the vat and up this chute several feet before it will go. A big sheep with its six months growth of wool full of water is mighty heavy. Especially at the end of a ten hour day. Ivor kept these sheep moving on up this chute into the draining pens, and changed the chute gate at the top to run the sheep into another drain pen when the first one was full, then turned them out of this pen into the big holding corral when the second drain pen was about full, so the first pen would be ready to receive wet sheep again. Some times when he was off during the gate changing etc., the sheep in the chute would turn around and d run back down into the vat, the only time they would jump into the dip.

This put a lot of extra work on me. To do our work, Rob and I had dipping hooks made like [a double hook -- UU -- sketch in original mss] fastened to a long handle, the center space was the center space was placed just behind the ears to push a sheep under, and the other two hooks were to hook around their head and pull them out of the dip. Ivor had one of these to use if necessary. Our record of 240,000 broke any dipping record ever made in Modena and we lost only seven sheep at the vat; a mortality record never even approached at any dipping vat in the history of the sheep industry. The sheep men were so pleased over this mortality record that they gave Will Lund a check for $100 bonus for us. Will said that every year before they had to send a truck up there two or three times a week to haul off the dead sheep.

I had quite a responsibility here of keeping sheep coming regularly so we would not have to wait for sheep and yet not have them brought in too soon. This took a lot of calculation and good timing. We made quite a little better than wages for that period on this job.

I sheared sheep here, too, several seasons before I went to work in the store. I also sheared one season at Casto [Canyon, near Panguitch] on the Sevier River when I lived at Hatch, and one season at Sullivan's Corral south of St. George. On this last job I just made enough to pay for my shearing machine and couldn't use it after buying it because of a crooked line shaft, so I went home broke, when Annie and the girls needed shoes and clothes and we were about out of flour.

Antone Neilson heard of this and came to our rescue by having me shingle his father's house. He gave me an order on the grist mill at St. George for 200 pounds of flour, and paid me cash for the balance, so I could buy the shoes and cloth for dresses. I have always had a high regard for Antone because of this kindness. This happened in the spring of 1921 when we first moved to Washington. I got other shingling and carpenter work soon after and when melons and grapes were ripe established a fruit stand on the highway south of the farm and we got along all right financially after that.

In one of my papers I mention ox teams. I think it only fitting that I picture and describe an ox yoke, and explain it. [See sketch in original] It looked something like this. No 1. is an eye bolt through the center into which a chain was hooked or fastened, the other end of the chain being attached to the wagon or what ever was being pulled. [Numbers] 2 & 2 were eye bolts in the under edge into which a forked chain with about a three-inch diameter ring in the center was fastened. The end of the wagon tongue going through this ring.

This forked chain being long enough to hang or loop down in the center enough to hold the tongue about 16 to 20 inches above the ground. This chain guided the wagon and was used only on the wheel yoke. The yokes or bows used on lead oxen didn't have these chains. No. 3 [see sketch] are the bows. These were made of oak, birch or service berry, from 3/4 to one inch in diameter and bent [when wet] in the shape of a U and held in that position until they dried. Holes were bored through the upper ends of these through which iron pins were inserted to hold them up in place to fit the neck of the ox. These bows were put up under the neck of the ox and through holes in the yoke after the yoke was laid on the neck of the ox.

Its purpose was to prevent the ox from backing out of the yoke. The yoke was made of a strong timber about four inches thick and eight or ten inches wide, and about five feet long. The timber must be straight grained and strong. The "pull" or point of insertion was the bump on top of the neck, just in front of the weathers or top of the shoulders. I've seen many balky horses, but never saw a balky ox. Ox yokes or bows are on display in museums, but I am probably on of the few men left who ever saw them in actual daily use. Lots of ox teams were used Escalante when I was a boy.

Another experience I had in Modena before I was married I have failed to tell. I nearly died of arsenic poisoning from loading a car of ore from the Savanic Mine about 90 miles south of St. George somewhere. Brig Lund had orders to empty the sacks making up this car load and send them back to the mine to be refilled with ore. A boxcar was spotted at the ore platform one day about eleven o'clock, a.m. so Brig and my brother Ed and I got dinner early and went to work on this car.

I had injured my knee some way a few days before and was quite lame, so Brig proposed that I stay in the car and empty the sacks and he and Ed would carry them in to me. We finished the car about sundown, and I had been feeling sick for an hour or more, and had a severe headache. We didn't know about the arsenic in the ore and attributed my condition to the need for food. My stomach hurt a little but I thought it was because of the long job since dinner so ate quite a hearty supper. But before we got the dishes washed,(we were batching in Modena, we three and Joe Farnsworth and the R.R. agent, Bob Martin.) I became very sick and my stomach hurt terribly. After a while I became sick enough to vomit and threw up my supper, and probably part of my dinner.

Brig looked up antidotes to poison and found that regular store tea was an antidote to arsenic poisoning, which we decided it was. So Brig made a cup of tea for me and after drinking it I felt easier. He made me stay in bed the next day, and I was quite weak for several days. However some good came of it. Brig refused to empty any more ore sacks, and the company found that the copper in the form of dust left in the sacks was worth more than the sacks cost new. After that all the sacks went into the furnace with the ore. Brig Lund was a true "diamond-in-the-rough". One of the finest men I ever knew. When Ed and I went there to work, he said he knew our father well, and knew that we were used to having prayers at night before going to bed, so we would adopt that custom there.

We did just that, regardless of who might be in the house at the time. After they bought the store Aunt Zill used to come up and stay for a while each summer. She was just like a mother to me. I hope I can associate with them in the next life.

Annie just reminded me that I hadn't said a word about cutting hair. I never went to barber school but learned to cut hair out of necessity. I started in the town of Hebron when I was 14 or 15 years of age. Some of the men and boys had been to Delamar to work and came home for Christmas with a two or three months growth of hair, and saw me cutting my father's hair, who had been out there with them, so they came and insisted that I cut their hair also. With their pleading and father coaxing I finally agreed to try. The attempt proved quite satisfactory so from then out I was the official tonsorial artist for Hebron.

The custom went to Enterprise with me and continued there until Frank Hunt went to barber school and got a license and set up a shop, then I quit except on rare occasions. I cut nearly ever man and boy's hair both at Hebron and Enterprise, from the bishop down. When we went to Hatch, the same condition existed there as did when I started at Hebron so I continued the practice. Annie says hardly a Sunday passed for years that I didn't cut one or more heads of hair before Sunday School. Friday afternoon was almost dedicated to it in all three places, and in the ten or 15 years I did it, I am sure I never received more than [a total of] $5.00 for it. I never made a charge, but once in a great while someone would slip me a quarter for it. I believe Bishop George A. Holt and Bishop Ross Lyman of Hatch always did this. I even shaved Jockey Hail once in Lee Adam's shop once in St. George.

Another thing I should tell about, although it shows a little of my Welsh temper, but I believe you will say there were extenuating circumstances. I went to the well at the Holt mine near my ranch north of Enterprise, as was my custom about three times a week, to get a load of water, and a sheep man pulled in by the well just ahead of me to water his team and fill his barrels. The well was 96 feet deep, equipped with a regular well bucket on each end of a rope, the rope being passed through a large pulley on the well-head frame.

I got off my wagon and drew water for this man to water his horses and fill two 50 gallon barrels and several kegs. When he was all fixed up he got on his wagon and drove about and I drove my wagon in by the well, thinking he would ad least offer to help me, as I had a team to water, and six 50 gallon barrels, two cream cans and two five-gallon kegs, but he drove right off and never looked back. About two weeks later when I got back to the ranch with my load of water this man had about a third of his sheep in my field about 100 yards from the house and was standing by watching the herd stringing into the field where the feed was good.

I drove into my yard with the water, put on the brake and tied my lines up and started over to take possession of the sheep, but before I got to them he sent his dog around them and run them out. The lower barbed wire on my fence was high enough that sheep could run under it. He had camped two nights east of my field so close that there was just room for his sheep to bed between his wagon and my fence, and some of the sheep fed in my field most of the night. I walked up to him and looked up at him, he was six feet tall, and asked him if he was going to keep his sheep out of my field. He was holding to the barrel of a 30-30 Winchester rifle with the butt on his foot. He said he would do as he pleased about that.

I said he would do as I pleased when I got through with him, and swung right at his jaw. He was looking for it and dodged and whirled around and came up with the muzzle of his gun in my face. I grabbed the gun and wrenched it out of his hand and he run, thinking I guess I would shoot him. I threw the gun away and took after him and grabbed his coat a time or two and tore a piece out of it, but finally got a solid hold and stopped him and begun to pummel him. The second lick I tore the lobe of one ear loose and he began to beg. I pummeled him good, then let him go with a promise to keep his sheep out of my field.

The herder told me the man ordered him to put the sheep in my field and he refused to do it, so the man, who was his boss, sent him for supplies and put the sheep in the field himself. When the herder got back the boss trailed the supply wagon behind the sheep wagon and drove five or six miles north of my ranch before he stopped. About a year later my brother, Jim, and I went hunting a boy who was lost between Modena and Kanarra. He left his father in Modena one morning and started on foot to Kanarra to see his mother. A week later he had not reached Kanarra, so the whole country was out looking for him.

Jim and I went down the east side of the Shoal Creek wash with the idea that we could pick up his tracks I the soft dirt if he had crossed that way. We reached a sheep camp at noon and stopped for dinner. This camp was six miles east of my ranch and after dinner the boss said he would like to go over in that cove, pointing toward my ranch, as it looked like good fall sheep range, but he was afraid to. Jim asked the cause of his fear and he said there was a great big fellow owned that ranch and that the man was pugilist.

Jim asked the source of the rumor and he said Wilford Webster told him and said that man gave Webster a terrible whipping. Jim kidded him a little about it then told him I owned the ranch. He looked at me in surprise, then said that had he known a little guy like me owned it he would have been over there long ago. I told him he was welcome to come over, but if he did and acted like Webster did he would get the same treatment. Then I told him what caused the trouble and he said I did exactly right.

In passing, I will say I have worn two pair of boxing gloves more than any man in Southern Utah. One pair on my hands and the other pair on my face. I had three brothers older than I that were all good boxers and they made me box with them. After two or three years I got so I didn't wear them on my face so much, but made the other fellow wear mine on his face part of the time.

I just thought of something else that may be of interest to my children, for whom this history is written. This pertains to the Book of Mormon. When we lived on my ranch at Old Hebron, Grace and Priscilla asked me to read the Book of Mormon to them, so every night, after they went to bed I went into their room and read to them from the Book of Mormon. When Priscilla was here last, she talked about it and said she remembered a lot of the incidents of the Book of Mormon when she began teaching it later in life just from hearing me read it.

Several times in my life I have been very glad that I held the Priesthood. One occasion was when I worked for H. J. Doolittle Co. in Lund, Utah. Grace was a baby and became very sick. One night she became worse and we believed she was at the gates of death. She seemed to be looking at something beyond this life. I anointed her head with consecrated oil and then sealed the anointing in the power of the Priesthood, and commanded the evil one to leave the place and not attempt to take her life. She went to sleep before I had finished, and the next day was like herself again.

We were married a little over seven years when she was born and just felt like we couldn't live without her. In fact we felt like she was given us as a result of faith. About a year before she was born Annie was blessed in the St. George Temple by temple ordinance workers and given a promise that she should become a mother.

Another occasion was when we lived at Old Hebron. Desma had the flue and became so sick that we were afraid, again, that we would lose her. I administered to her again only this time I commanded the evil one by the power of the Priesthood and in the name of the Lord to depart and never return. She got well at once and has never had a serious sick spell since that I remember of.

Grace is now the mother of seven children, the oldest one being on a mission for the Church in Colorado. On an other occasion, Priscilla was down with typhoid fever, and was very sick. Billy Truman was on his ranch then as it was in the summer. He came over and we administered to her and the fever seemed to break immediately and she was soon all right. Billy also administered to me once, and I was healed almost instantly. In this case one joint in my neck became enlarged and affected my arms. They would go to sleep in the night and I would get up and walk the floor and whip them on my legs and shake them to get the blood to circulating again.

So I just went over to his place and stated the trouble and asked him to administer to me. He anointed the crown of my head and this enlarged joint with consecrated oil and blessed me and commanded what ever was wrong to be corrected. I felt something begin to move down through my left shoulder blade and seemed to pass out of my body. I have never had the trouble since and in a short time that enlarged joint was normal again. There is power in the holy Melchizedek Priesthood.

I wrote my son-in-law [Whitney Cude] when he was Fire Control Fist Class on the light cruiser, St. Louis in world war two and told him he held the priesthood which was more powerful than any instrument of destruction man could invent. He said a shell came so close to him once it tore the shirt off his back and the concussion knocked him unconscious, and that when he regained consciousness he was 30 feet from where he was standing. When the typhoon struck his ship he had just come out of the bath room on to the deck. He said he saw an upright pipe going by and grabbed it, locking his fingers together. He said he whipped in the wind like a rag, and it felt like his arms would be pulled off, but he escaped. Several men were blown overboard and never found.

When the flu struck Enterprise there were only three or four men who didn't get it. I was on of them, and we were kept busy doing chores and running errands for those who were down. I mad and helped make and trim a lot of coffins both at this time and when the typhoid fever epidemic hit Enterprise. I didn't have the flu until practically everyone else had gotten over it. I milked cows, fed stock and chopped wood for about five families beside my own and bought supplies at the store, and mailed letters for them. I milked six or seven cows at my brother Ed's place that were all high producers, separated his milk, shipped his cream, fed cows, calves, pigs and three horses, and kept his stables cleaned out besides milking a cow or two for three or four other families and doing my own chores and milking.

I never went into a house, but conversed with them every day through an open window. The day we were making the last coffin some young men who had just been released out of Quarantine came into the shop and I guess I caught the flu from them. Anyway we moved up to our ranch two days later and I started with the flu. Its a wonder it didn't kill me because I thought I couldn't go to bed. It was planting time and I had no ground plowed, and had wood to chop, cows to milk and feed, horses, calves and pigs to feed, etc. I plowed every day and when my back got to hurting too bad I got off the sulky plow and leaned over the seat with my back to the sun until it felt better, then went to plowing again. It was so late and the ground had got so dry that [we] raised but very little crop that year.

It was this summer that I broke some of my ribs. I went out in the hills NW, of Hebron to get some barn posts. I had chopped about 10 or 12 cedar trees about 12 inches in diameter at the but. One of these was close to the wagon, so I hitched the team up and loaded this one on the running gears of the wagon (no box, no rack). I was driving to the next tree and was standing up so I could see better with one foot on the front bolster and the other foot on this post when one front wheel hit an old stump concealed in the brush, and this threw me in the air and I lit on the front wheel on my right side.

I sat down for a few minutes and my side quit hurting and felt numb, so I got up and finished loading the posts or logs and started home. When I got about half way I crossed a rocky spot in the road and this brought that side to life again and it pained me very much, and from then on home I suffered a lot of pain. When I got to the ranch I could scarcely get off the wagon for the pain it caused me to move. I tried to unhitch the team and couldn't, as using my right hand was so painful I almost fainted, therefore Annie and Grace had to unhitch and unharness the team and put them in the stable.

I went to the house and tried to wash, but just couldn't do it for the pain it caused in my side. I slept but very little that night. We talked of taking me to a doctor the next morning but the nearest one was [in] St. George or Cedar City, and I was sure I couldn't stand the ride. By then we had discovered that four or five lower ribs were broken under my right arm and the cartilage that holds the ribs together in front was broken off so that a section about the size of my hand had "fallen in" so to speak. Early that morning Lance Readhead came to the house to see if I had seen some horses he had on the range north of my ranch, and he told me what to do.

He had suffered a similar accident a few years ago in Arizona and the doctor had him lie face down and eat bread and milk and other bulky food and drink water often to keep his stomach full and exert a little pressure on the ribs from the inside. This would hold them out in place until they knit or grew together again. We just put a mattress out under the trees and I laid on that night and day for about a week, and it worked. I had to favor that side for a month or so, but before the summer was over it got all right.

I have overlooked telling how close I came to having my bones now lying at the bottom of the Old Hold mine north of Enterprise, under 100 feet of water. I walked down there one evening to get my milk cows but it was a little too early to bring them home. I ad been told that one could see the water running across the mine shaft at the bottom of the double compartment shaft about 120 feet down, and that by sticking a short piece of candle to a small block and lighting it, and placing it near the SW corner of the shaft it would float across the shaft. I knew efforts had been made to pump this water out by several big mining companies to get to the high grade silver around the old hoist house at the top of the shaft. I found some pieces of candles and some small blocks. There was what appeared to be a good ladder down this shaft, so I decided to go down and make the test. The water had broken into the mine about a hundred feet above the bottom of the shaft. I went down without incident, and after playing a while with the blocks and candles and establishing the truthfulness of the rumors, I started to climb back up the ladder. But before I got to the top of the first section the ladder broke and I fell back but stayed on the shelf at the bottom of the double compartment shaft by hooking one foot behind the foot of the ladder.

I tried to climb the wall of the shaft up to the solid ladder, but couldn't. A mine bucket was hanging down the shaft to within about a foot of the water, but I wasn't sure the cable was fastened solid at the top. I got a piece of the ladder which had some nails in it and hooked the cable and pulled over where I could get hold of it. I tested it and found it would support my weight so uttering a prayer for help I began climbing this 5/8 inch cable. I thought I could swing myself over to the solid [ladder] when I reached it but couldn't so I had to climb the entire distance on the cable.

My shoulders, arms and hands got so tired when near the top that I was afraid I couldn't make it. I had noticed the cable was frayed about 20 feet below me and knew if I slid back down the cable my hands would be torn to shreds, so I made a super-human effort and by the help of the Lord, finally reached the top and rolled onto the cover of the shaft. I was completely exhausted and had to lay here a little while before I could take the cows home.

Index

Printed in Great Britain
by Amazon

39185396R00059